Henry James's

THE PORTRAIT OF A LADY

Bloom's

NOTES

CURRENTLY AVAILABLE

The Adventures of Huckleberry Finn
Mark Twain

Aeneid
Vergil

Animal Farm
George Orwell

The Autobiography of Malcolm X
Alex Haley & Malcolm X

Beowulf

Billy Budd, Benito Cereno, & Bartleby the Scrivener
Herman Melville

Brave New World
Aldous Huxley

The Catcher in the Rye
J. D. Salinger

Crime and Punishment
Fyodor Dostoevsky

The Crucible
Arthur Miller

Death of a Salesman
Arthur Miller

The Divine Comedy (Inferno)
Dante

A Farewell to Arms
Ernest Hemingway

Frankenstein
Mary Shelley

The Grapes of Wrath
John Steinbeck

Great Expectations
Charles Dickens

The Great Gatsby
F. Scott Fitzgerald

Gulliver's Travels
Jonathan Swift

Hamlet
William Shakespeare

Heart of Darkness & The Secret Sharer
Joseph Conrad

Henry IV, Part One
William Shakespeare

I Know Why the Caged Bird Sings
Maya Angelou

Iliad
Homer

Invisible Man
Ralph Ellison

Jane Eyre
Charlotte Brontë

Julius Caesar
William Shakespeare

King Lear
William Shakespeare

Lord of the Flies
William Golding

Macbeth
William Shakespeare

A Midsummer Night's Dream
William Shakespeare

Moby-Dick
Herman Melville

Native Son
Richard Wright

Nineteen Eighty-Four
George Orwell

Odyssey
Homer

Oedipus Plays
Sophocles

Of Mice and Men
John Steinbeck

The Old Man and the Sea
Ernest Hemingway

Othello
William Shakespeare

Paradise Lost
John Milton

Pride and Prejudice
Jane Austen

The Red Badge of Courage
Stephen Crane

Romeo and Juliet
William Shakespeare

The Scarlet Letter
Nathaniel Hawthorne

Silas Marner
George Eliot

The Sun Also Rises
Ernest Hemingway

A Tale of Two Cities
Charles Dickens

Tess of the D'Urbervilles
Thomas Hardy

To Kill a Mockingbird
Harper Lee

Uncle Tom's Cabin
Harriet Beecher Stowe

Wuthering Heights
Emily Brontë

VIVA

Bloom's

NOTES

Henry James's

THE PORTRAIT OF A LADY

Edited and with an Introduction by

HAROLD BLOOM

Viva Books Private Limited

New Delhi • Mumbai • Chennai • Kolkata • Bangalore • Hyderabad

First Indian Edition 2007

VIVA BOOKS PRIVATE LIMITED

- 4737/23 Ansari Road, Daryaganj, New Delhi 110 002
  E-mail: vivadelhi@vivagroupindia.net, Tel. 42242200
- Plot No. 76, Service Industries, Shirvane, Sector 1, Nerul, Navi Mumbai 400 706
  E-mail: vivamumbai@vivagroupindia.net, Tel. 27721273, 27721274
- Jamals Fazal Chambers, 26 Greams Road, Chennai 600 006
  E-mail: vivachennai@vivagroupindia.net, Tel. 28290304, 28294241
- B-103, Jindal Towers, 21/1A/3 Darga Road, Kolkata 700 017
  E-mail: vivakolkata@vivagroupindia.net, Tel. 22836381, 22816713
- 7, Sovereign Park Apartments, 56-58, K. R. Road, Basavanagudi, Bangalore 560 004
  E-mail: vivabangalore@vivagroupindia.net, Tel.26607409, 26607410
- 101-102 Mughal Marc Apartments, 3-4-637 to 641, Narayanguda, Hyderabad 500 029
  E-mail: vivahyderabad@vivagroupindia.net, Tel. 27564481, 27564482

Published by arrangement with

Facts on File, Inc.
132 West 31st Street
New York NY 10001
USA

ISBN 81-309-0443-8

Published by Vinod Vasishtha for Viva Books Private Limited, 4737/23 Ansari Road
New Delhi 110 002. Printed and bound at Anand Sons, Delhi.

Contents

User's Guide

This volume is designed to present biographical, critical, and bibliographical information on the author and the work. Following Harold Bloom's editor's note and introduction are a detailed biography of the author, discussing major life events and important literary works. Then follows a thematic and structural analysis of the work, which traces significant themes, patterns, and motifs. An annotated list of characters supplies brief information on the chief characters in the work.

A selection of critical extracts, derived from previously published material by leading critics, then follows. The extracts consist of statements by the author, early reviews of the work, and later evaluations up to the present. These items are arranged chronologically by date of first publication. A bibliography of the author's writings (including a complete list of all books written, cowritten, edited, and translated), a list of additional books and articles on the author and the work, and an index of themes conclude the volume.

Harold Bloom is Sterling Professor of the Humanities at Yale University and Henry W. and Albert A. Berg Professor of English at the New York University Graduate School. He is the author of twenty books and the editor of more than thirty anthologies of literary criticism.

Professor Bloom's works include *Shelley's Mythmaking* (1959), *The Visionary Company* (1961), *Blake's Apocalypse* (1963), *Yeats* (1970), *A Map of Misreading* (1975), *Kabbalah and Criticism* (1975), and *Agon: Towards a Theory of Revisionism* (1982). *The Anxiety of Influence* (1973) sets forth Professor Bloom's provocative theory of the literary relationships between the great writers and their predecessors. His most recent books include *The American Religion* (1992), *The Western Canon* (1994), and *Omens of Millennium: The Gnosis of Angels, Dreams, and Resurrection* (1996).

Professor Bloom earned his Ph.D. from Yale University in 1955 and has served on the Yale faculty since then. He is a 1985 MacArthur Foundation Award recipient and served as the Charles Elkot Norton Professor of Poetry at Harvard University in 1987–88. He is currently the editor of other Chelsea House series in literary criticism, including MAJOR LITERARY CHARACTERS, MODERN CRITICAL VIEWS, and WOMEN WRITERS OF ENGLISH AND THEIR WORKS.

Editor's Note

My Introduction addresses the enigmas of Isabel Archer's intial choice of Osmond, and her decision to return to him.

The critical extracts begin with John Hay's early appreciation of the "portrait" of Isabel, and go on to Joseph Warren Beach's analysis of the heroine as a spiritual quester. Graham Greene, James's disciple as a novelist, reflects upon Isabel's stance in the architecture of the book, while the English critic F. R. Leavis sets the heroine's context by examining some of the figures who surround her.

In Dorothy Van Ghent's view, Isabel's fate is a version of our Fall from Eden, after which the distinguished American critic Richard Poirier centers upon the voice narrating the novel. Leon Edel, James's biographer, finds the model for Isabel in the novelist's long-dead cousin Minny Temple, while Walter Wright relates the heroine to the American girls of James's earlier works.

J.I.M. Stewart emphasizes Isabel's drive for freedom, after which Elisabeth Carey points out the role of money in the book. Laurence Holland shrewdly explores the analogues between Henry James's self-recognitions as an artist and Isabel's attempts to realize herself.

The metaphor of the bolted door, pervasive in the *Portrait*, is analyzed by John Rodenback, while Sister Lucy Schneider, C.S.J., finds a potential return to religious faith in Isabel's decision to reject Goodwood. Nina Baym illuminates James's revisions of Isabel Archer, after which Elizabeth Allen shows the concern of Isabel for the world of appearances.

Tony Tanner brilliantly conveys the differences between Isabel and her betrayers, Osmond and Madame Merle, while Deborah Esch shows how subtly James's own self-criticism alters the *Portrait*.

Change and the sense of death in the novel are chronicled by William Veeder, after which Lyall Powers meditates upon Isabel's American innocence. Jonathan Warren considers the temporal limitations of Isabel's idealistic quest, while Kelly Cannon speculates that Ralph Touchett is at least pragmatically impotent, and so capable only of a voyeurism in regard to his beloved Isabel.

Introduction

HAROLD BLOOM

Henry James was an endlessly fecund novelist and short-story writer, and character-portraiture was one of his many superb skills. When I think of James's men, women, and children, my thoughts do not turn first to Lambert Strether in *The Ambassadors*, or to Milly Theale in *The Wings of the Dove*, but always to Isabel Archer in *The Portrait of a Lady*. James could not rival Shakespeare as a creator of personality; even Isabel cannot compete with Falstaff, Hamlet, Rosalind, Iago, Lear, Macbeth, Cleopatra, and all the other figures who walk off Shakespeare's stage into our imaginative lives. But Isabel Archer comes closest to Shakespearean dimensions; she has proved almost endless to meditation for critics and other readers. Why does she marry Osmond, and again, why does she return to him, in the novel's enigmatic close?

Isabel Archer has elements in her of Jamesian self-portraiture, but she lacks his comic sense and his stubborn (though highly individual) realism. She is an Emersonian Transcendentalist of the highest seriousness, and her quest is for self-reliance, the Emersonian secular religion. Lee Clark Mitchell, in a recent essay (*Raritan*, Winter 1998), argues that Isabel manifests something of the Shakespearean power to read us more fully than we can read her:

> This artful presentation of Isabel as portrait and plot, object and subject, end and means, forms James's first great investigation of the way in which selfhood is produced as a mutual process of cross reading. To put it that way, however, renders the issues less compelling than they are, especially since the reader is coerced into questioning responses that align him or her with characters in the novel. Recall Daniel Touchett's query to Ralph before making the bequest that will change her life: "Isabel's a sweet thing: but do you think she's so good as that?" His son responds succinctly that "She's as good as her best opportunities." Indeed it is *because* she seems larger than "her best opportunities" that we join the characters in imagining possibilities that expose our

> own manipulations, our own incorrigible impulse toward plot and plotting that is everywhere both celebrated and critiqued by the novel. It is something of a truism to claim that the portrait of Isabel is as well a test of our imaginative abilities and novelistic powers. What will she do? We continue to ask, and the judgments we provide end by judging us. But what is more troubling is the degree to which Isabel's hesitation about this eminently human, ultimately exhausting process leads her simply to withdraw. Indeed, one way to think of the end of the novel is of Isabel finally escaping the frame, evading those of us who ask what she will do. It almost seems that she has decided to abandon the novel itself, as if she saw us watching her and refused any more to submit to our plots. That, of course, is the one way to ensure we persist in making them up.

Mitchell implicitly asserts that Isabel, like Falstaff or Hamlet or Cleopatra, is an instance of what we mean by the popular metaphor "larger than life." Yet there is a puzzle (as Mitchell knows) in such an assertion; we do not doubt the intensity of Isabel's consciousness or the power of her character, but James cannot give us a full and direct sense of her personality. She is always mediated for us, primarily by the narrator, secondarily by the other figures in the novel. We never achieve the closeness to her that only James himself enjoys, which is another hint as to why James failed as a playwright. James has such art at imitation that we accept his vision of the infinite possibilities available for his heroine. If we did not believe in Isabel's potential for greatness, then the book would fail. No sympathetic reader doubts Isbael's capaciousness of soul; James persuades us that magnificence abides in her, even though we cannot establish just how the glory of her being yet will manifest itself. From the start, we are shown Isabel as a marvelous dreamer, and we never quite accept James's dark irony that the aesthetic *poseur*, Osmond, should be her free choice, her attempt to realize the dream. James subtly never allows her a truly imaginative choice; all her admirers are inadequate to her superb sense of possibility. Ralph Touchett, the best of them, is too ill to become her husband, while Warburton represents too socially closed a world. The absurdly named Caspar Goodwood is nevertheless her authentic option, but the male force of his passion threatens Isabel's autonomy, and she fears the obliteration of aspects of her self in so consuming a marriage. What remains is Osmond, a parody of both Emerson's idealism and of Walter Pater's aestheticism. Isabel's catastrophe is the cost of her confirmation as an Emersonian quester.

Shakespeare's women almost invariably marry down, in a pattern that makes feminist criticism of Shakespeare rather redundant. Isabel spectacularly fails in her initial judgment of Osmond, and yet James is more in the American tradition than the Shakespearean when he allows Isabel to be blind. Hawthorne, James's American original, had given us the wonderful Hester Prynne, whose two-object choices were her Satanic husband, Chillingworth, and her desperate, irresolute lover, Dimmesdale. With each heroine, her mistakes about life are essential to the novelist's art, but there is a crucial difference between Hester and Isabel. Hawthorne persuades us of Hester's sexual power, of her drive for more life, while James makes us wonder why Isabel's palpable vitality of spirit is so fearful, not of sexual expression, but the consequences of yielding fully to Goodwood's passion. It may be that James identified too closely with Isabel; Hawthorne loves his Hester, but knows his distance from her, because he conceives her as a tragic protagonist. Isabel Archer ought not to be seen even as tragicomic; as an Emersonian, she will always demand victory, however often she is self-defeated. Mistaken in her initial choice of Osmond, she nevertheless is truest to herself in returning to her ruined marriage. Her self-trust has been shaken, but hardly obliterated; essentially she returns to herself, in order to work out the consequences of her idealistic blunder.

I am not being upbeat about this, because Isabel is not reaffirming her earlier choice, but rather she proudly asserts the continuity of her own spirit. Nietzsche says that the will's revenge against time is to affirm again: *thus* I willed it. James will not prophesy for us Isabel's ultimate destination, but clearly she and Osmond will not be at peace, and if there is war, then she will win. Such a victory would be only a minor aspect of her solitude, which is to say: of her freedom. The greatness of *The Portrait of a Lady*, and of Isabel Archer, is finally James's own greatness: the achieved sense of the self's triumph over all contingencies, including those created by the self's own errors.

Biography of Henry James

(1843–1916)

Henry James, Jr., was born in New York City on April 15, 1843. His father, Henry James, Sr., was a prominent figure in social and intellectual circles; his mother, Mary Robertson Walsh James, was from a wealthy, staunchly Presbyterian, Albany, New York, family. Henry, Jr., would remember her as "the keystone of the arch" of the family. James's older brother, William, was a philosopher, psychologist, and Harvard professor; his younger sister, Alice, also became a writer. The James children were privately tutored in New York and traveled in Europe from 1855 through 1860, when the family lived in London, Switzerland, France, and Germany. Intellectual growth was always the educational focus in the James household. In 1858 and 1859 Henry and his brother studied painting in Newport, Rhode Island, with the painter John LaFarge before returning to Switzerland and Germany.

In 1862, at age nineteen, James entered the Law School at Harvard, the same year he sustained an injury, most likely to his back, that kept him from service in the Civil War. In 1865, James began publishing sketches, critical reviews, and short stories in prominent literary magazines such as the *Atlantic Monthly* and the *North American Review*. In 1875, *A Passionate Pilgrim and Other Tales*, a collection of short stories, was published and *Roderick Hudson*, his first novel, was serialized in the *Atlantic*. James spent much time in Paris during this period and came to know Flaubert and Turgenev. French and Russian realism and naturalism would have a profound influence upon James's style. By 1876, James had settled in London, and he would make his home in Europe for the rest of his life.

James's best early works are *The American* (1877), *Daisy Miller* (1879), *The Portrait of a Lady*, his finest novel of this period and one in which the presence of evil is explored

(1881), and *The Princess Casamassima* (1886). With *The Tragic Muse* (1890), James's style became increasingly complex, the psychological motivations of his characters more intense and more often evil. The development of this style may be traced through *The Pupil* (1891), *The Spoils of Poynton* (1897), *What Maisie Knew* (1897), *The Turn of the Screw* (1898), *The Awkward Age* (1899), and *The Sacred Fount* (1901). James wrote his most important novels after 1900: *The Wings of the Dove* (1902), *The Ambassadors* (1903), and *The Golden Bowl* (1904).

In 1884, James published an essay in *Longman's* magazine that we know as "The Art of Fiction." This work defends the novel form as a legitimate work of art and remains one of the most important studies on the art of writing fiction. To James, the novel is, as much as poetry, a possessor of symbolic value. Many authors have claimed James as an influence, including D. H. Lawrence, James Joyce, Joseph Conrad, Edith Wharton (with whom he was great friends), Virginia Woolf, Willa Cather, and T. S. Eliot. F. Scott Fitzgerald, Ernest Hemingway, and William Faulkner are less directly his descendants.

In 1915, in protest against America's neutrality at the beginning of World War I, Henry James became a British subject. He died in London on February 28, 1916. ✤

Thematic and Structural Analysis

Chapter one of *The Portrait of a Lady* opens upon three gentlemen at a typical afternoon tea ceremony at Gardencourt, the English country house of the Touchett family. Engaged in witty conversation are Mr. Daniel Touchett, a retired American banker; his sickly and unattractive son, Ralph; and Lord Warburton, a handsome and bored man of thirty-five, dressed in riding clothes. This carefully constructed scene is typical of James's style and technique. The tea ceremony, the imposing and historical English manor house with its ethos of permanence and quality, and the intrusion of an ambitious and astute American into the scene throws into relief the themes of the novel that form around issues of class and history, money and position, independence and entrapment, and the social aspirations of Americans in Europe. Mrs. Lydia Touchett, returning from a visit to her sister in America, arrives with her niece, Isabel Archer. The young woman seems to meet the description given in Mrs. Touchett's telegram, that she is "quite independent." By the end of the **second chapter**, Lord Warburton is intrigued by Isabel, speculating to Ralph that she is his "idea of an interesting woman." The eventual ironic reversal of Isabel's assertion of independence and of her circumstances is one of the major themes of the novel.

Chapters three and **four** provide information about Isabel's past and background and about the "many oddities" of her maternal aunt, Lydia Touchett. Upon meeting her aunt at her Albany, New York, home, Isabel remarks thoughtlessly, "You must be our crazy Aunt Lydia." With that remark, the two immediately become friends, and Lydia decides to take her niece back to England. Isabel recognizes this as an opportunity for adventure and new experience. Her adoring and indulgent father is dead and her sister, popular with the young men and socially successful, overshadows the intelligent but bookish Isabel. Her older married sister is pleased that Isabel will have this "chance to develop" by visiting Europe. In **chapter four**, James emphasizes Isabel's capacity for imaginative as well as clear and realistic thinking. Caspar Goodwood is introduced; he is a persistent though disappointed admirer of Isabel's who will figure importantly in later chapters.

The design of James's novel begins to unfold in **chapter five**. We learn the circumstances of the Touchett family's arrival in England from Vermont and of the weak health of Ralph Touchett. He realizes that he will never fully recover from a weakness in his lungs, and that his life will be short. He is not a self-pitying character, however. He decides to live his life as happily as possible, and his devotion to his cousin Isabel is always generous. James foreshadows several developments in the fifth chapter. Ralph travels to Rome each winter for his health, returning to England before the heat becomes oppressive. Yet, in the thirty-eighth and thirty-ninth chapters, Ralph will remain in England for Isabel's sake, knowing it will be fatal to him. The ghost Isabel will see in chapter fifty-five is foreshadowed when Ralph tells her that ghosts may be seen only after one has "suffered greatly" and "gained some miserable knowledge."

Chapter six opens with an impression of Isabel through the narrator's eyes and through those of her contemporaries: She is thought to be "a young person of many theories . . . [caring] for knowledge that was tinged with the unfamiliar." Her aunt concludes she is writing a novel; her friends describe her as versed in the classics, "a prodigy of learning" (here James echoes an eighteenth-century comedy of manners). Isabel is innocent of the evil in the world and is concerned chiefly with all that is pleasing and proper. We gain more insight into Isabel's character by her admiration for the journalist Henrietta Stackpole, whom she perceives to be happy and able to take care of herself without getting married. Isabel's friendship with Mr. Touchett becomes stronger; her energy and naturalness remind him of a young Lydia. Because Isabel, throughout the novel, never fulfills Touchett's wish that she ask him for something, we are prepared for the ease with which he later provides her with a large inheritance.

Ralph realizes, to his dismay, that his father will soon die (**chapter seven**). Father and son have been close; he has felt his father needed him in a way his independent mother did not. Although not romantically in love with Isabel, he wants to help her fulfill her expectations of life. Lord Warburton visits Gardencourt; Isabel, happy to be in his company, wants to remain with him after her aunt decides to retire for the evening. Mrs. Touchett advises Isabel that, in England, a young woman cannot remain alone with a gentleman under such circumstances. The contrast in attitudes throughout the novel reiterates James's theme of the American in Europe.

In **chapter eight**, Lord Warburton makes Mrs. Touchett and Ralph promise to bring Isabel to visit his estate, Lockleigh. He describes his family and his politics, convincing Isabel that he is "a nobleman of the newest pattern, a reformer, a radical, a contemner of ancient ways." Mr. Touchett offers Isabel a different perspective, shared by Ralph, observing that such men, while "they are very conscientious, . . . [t]heir radical views are a kind of amusement;" their "progressive ideas are about their biggest luxury." Warburton has money, position in Parliament, good taste, and is well-liked; but both Mr. Touchett and Ralph feel pity for him.

Isabel questions Lord Warburton's sisters, the Misses Molyneaux, about his political opinions (**chapter nine**), but they seem only to misunderstand them. Through their answers we learn more of his fine character and natural nobility. Warburton will stand as the perfect marriage choice that Isabel will later refuse. In this chapter, and throughout the novel, Isabel views the possibility of deep emotional attachment as a danger to her privacy and independence. She reacts with panic but also with the courage to make decisions she feels are necessary.

Newspaperwoman Henrietta Stackpole comes to Europe on assignment for the *Interviewer* and Isabel, on Mr. Touchett's insistence, invites her to stay at the Touchett estate (**chapter ten**). Henrietta begins writing an article about Gardencourt, which Isabel asks Henrietta to discontinue for the reason that the Touchetts would consider it a breach of hospitality. Henrietta complies, but laments sacrificing such a beautiful subject. Henrietta is a distinctively American character, espousing a candid American point of view in every conversation. Her honesty seems to expose an essential meaninglessness of the European customs and rituals she sees. Her concern is for Isabel, and she will later press Isabel to come to some sort of understanding with Caspar Goodwood in **chapter eleven**.

A note from Caspar Goodwood, delivered to Isabel at Gardencourt (**chapter eleven**), asserts that although she had dismissed him three months earlier, he had not given up his pursuit of her. He asks only that she see him for half an hour. As she folds the note, she looks up to find Lord Warburton standing before her. In dramatic contrast to this scene, Isabel, in the novel's final chapter, will look up to find Caspar Goodwood standing before her as she thinks of Lord Warburton.

On this occasion, as Isabel looks at Warburton (**chapter twelve**), she realizes that he is about to propose. He tells her that he loved her immediately and asks her to marry him. Isabel, although honored, carefully refuses him. Her ambition is not to marry well, but to live well, free to explore life's possibilities as she imagines them. Warburton claims to love her because she is a woman of ideas, yet also admits that he is afraid of her capacity for ideas and of her remarkable mind.

Isabel's rejection of Warburton, in the next chapter, will be questioned at many points in the novel. Isabel confides to her uncle the details of Warburton's proposal and of her intended refusal (**chapter thirteen**). Afterward, she has thoughts of Caspar Goodwood, though not in regard to marriage. Goodwood is a strong and capable man whose persistent pursuit of Isabel seems to threaten her sense of her own freedom. Before answering Goodwood's note, she writes to Warburton that she will not marry him.

Henrietta, worried that Isabel might yet indeed marry a European, urges Ralph to invite Goodwood to Gardencourt in hopes that a marriage may yet be arranged (**chapter thirteen**). Caspar refuses, confirming Ralph's feeling that such an invitation had been in poor taste. When Lord Warburton comes to Gardencourt the next day (**chapter fourteen**), he asks Isabel if there is another man in her life. She insists that there is not and tries to explain: "It is that I can't escape my fate. . . . I can never be happy in any extraordinary way; not by turning away, by separating myself [from] life. From the usual chances and dangers, from what most people know and suffer."

Ralph, Isabel, and Henrietta travel to London (**chapter fifteen**) for sightseeing, and Isabel, although under the watchful and concerned eyes of Ralph Touchett, regains her sense of freedom. Henrietta visits some young American friends she has met in London, leaving Ralph and Isabel alone for an evening. He asks Isabel why she refused Lord Warburton, but as the conversation concludes he can determine only that the greater world of adventure and experience interests her more. Another manifestation of Isabel's need for independence and for solitude is her gentle refusal to dine with Ralph. As she sits at her table in the hotel dining room, reading a book she has brought from Gardencourt, the waiter delivers Caspar Goodwood's calling card; she agrees to see him (**chapter sixteen**). Isabel tells him, bluntly, that he simply does not fit into her plans at the moment. Although hurt, Caspar persists until Isabel requests that he neither write nor visit her for two years. He tells her he will return to America immediately, but he fears that she will marry someone else. She assures him that she will not, adding that she has already rejected a nobleman with a great fortune. Caspar vows to return to see her at the end of two years, although Isabel promises him nothing. Ironically, in her marriage to Gilbert Osmond, she will lose the freedom that she might have retained in a marriage to Caspar.

Henrietta Stackpole returns to find Isabel recovering from her encounter with Caspar, relieved that her sense of personal liberty remains intact (**chapter seventeen**). Henrietta accepts an invitation to stay with friends in London in order to observe aspects of British life interesting to a journalist. Before departing, she tells Ralph that Isabel has refused Caspar and of her concern for her friend's future. Ralph receives word from his mother that his father is gravely ill, and Isabel returns with him to Gardencourt. They barely speak on the train trip (**chapter eighteen**). James achieves in this scene his intention of "the maximum of intensity with the minimum of words."

Later at Gardencourt, when Isabel comes downstairs to find Madame Merle playing Schubert on the piano, they begin a relationship that will affect Isabel profoundly: "She was in a word a woman of ardent impulses, kept in admirable order. What an ideal combination! thought Isabel." Isabel's meeting with Madame Merle is the turning point of the novel. That is, by eventually putting Isabel together with Gilbert Osmond, Madame Merle shapes the plot. Mr. Touchett urges Ralph to marry Isabel; instead, Ralph convinces his father to leave to Isabel half of his own inheritance, in order that she be rich enough to fulfill all her dreams.

As has been noted by critics of *The Portrait of a Lady*, **chapter nineteen** ends the first of the novel's three sections. The themes presented so far are structured around Warburton's proposal to Isabel; Isabel's rejection of that proposal; and the death of Daniel Touchett. These stories foreshadow as they construct the rest of the novel: We understand Isabel's character and the desires that motivate her decisions; the major characters and their relationships with Isabel (with the exception of Gilbert Osmond) are established; and the difficulties of the American in Europe is established as one of the novel's themes. The chapter concludes with the death of Daniel Touchett and Isabel becomes an heiress.

Madame Merle becomes aware of Isabel's inheritance in **chapter twenty** and decides that the young heiress would be an appropriate wife for Gilbert Osmond. Henrietta Stackpole, who joins Mrs. Touchett and Isabel in Paris where they travel after the death of Mr. Touchett, cautions Isabel against the influence of those who may be interested in her sizable inheritance. Isabel and her aunt travel to San Remo, Italy, to visit Ralph, who gives Isabel needed advice about the condition of having money (**chapter twenty-one**): "Live as you like best, and your character will form itself. Most things are good for you, the exceptions are very rare, and a comfortable income is not one of them. . . . It's out of all reason, the number of things you think wrong. Spread your wings; rise above the ground. It's never wrong to do that." Italy captures Isabel's imagination as she walks along the shore of the Mediterranean with Ralph, and she thinks of the future. Thoughts of the past include the certainty that Caspar Goodwood will write to her in another year and a half, and the hope that Lord Warburton will someday marry. Her pride will not allow her to think that Caspar may, in that time, find another, nor that she might feel jealousy if Warburton did.

By **chapter twenty-two**, Mr. Touchett has been dead for six months. This chapter introduces Gilbert Osmond, a handsome, intelligent, and indolent man of forty, and his young daughter, Pansy, who is on a visit to her father from the convent in Rome where she has lived since early childhood. Madame Merle is an intimate friend of Osmond and has come to his villa, near Florence. Osmond is a man of refined tastes and little money, and Madame Merle engages in a subtle plot to bring Osmond and Mrs. Touchett's rich, twenty-three-year-old niece together. In Florence at the invitation of Mrs. Touchett, Madame Merle invites Osmond to visit when Isabel will be present (**chapter twenty-three**). Osmond, in turn, invites Isabel to visit him and to meet his daughter. Although Ralph does not trust Madame Merle, he thinks that Isabel will come to no harm in her company.

At Osmond's hilltop home, Isabel meets his sister, the Countess Gemini. Isabel finds Gilbert Osmond to be cultured and refined (**chapter twenty-four**). He shows her his many objets d'art, and she is intimidated by his superior appreciation of these things and reluctant to express her opinions; she fears appearing foolish to him or perhaps to herself. He shows Isabel the view from the garden terrace and invites her to visit again. During their conversation, another takes place between the Countess Gemini and Madame Merle (**chapter twenty-five**). The Countess is aware of Madame Merle's and her brother's plan to lure Isabel into marriage, and she does not approve. She likes Isabel and sees clearly that Osmond and Madame Merle are only after Isabel's money. She knows that her brother will make a bad husband. Although Isabel, at this point, thinks the Countess Gemini to be trivial, stupid, and vain, she will be revealed later in the novel as far more shrewd in her understanding of the characters of her brother and Madame Merle.

By **chapter twenty-six**, Mrs. Touchett is uneasy that Gilbert Osmond has visited Isabel five times in two weeks. She consults Ralph, who reassures his mother that nothing will interfere with Isabel's plan to see and experience the world. She next turns to Madame Merle, who affects surprise and offers to question Osmond about his intentions, while carefully emphasizing his good taste and his lovely daughter. Isabel sees in Osmond neither artifice nor questionable intentions. Pansy's innocence complements the picture Isabel has of the girl's father.

Visiting Rome with Henrietta Stackpole and Ralph (**chapter twenty-seven**), Isabel is briefly alone in the Roman Forum and is surprised to see Lord Warburton approach. He, too, is surprised, and admits that he has been traveling since she refused him. Later, they meet Gilbert Osmond, and Warburton asks Ralph about Osmond's relationship with Isabel: "Is he a good fellow?" "No, he's not," Ralph replies. Both men know that Isabel will decide for herself.

Lord Warburton sees Isabel and Osmond in a box at the opera the next evening (**chapter twenty-eight**). He speaks with them briefly, then leaves, alone. Isabel remarks to Osmond on Warburton's gentlemanly character. It pleases Osmond to know that he may marry a woman who has rejected a man of Warburton's class and distinction. Osmond charms all whom he must and, by **chapter twenty-nine**, he has overcome the reservations even of Ralph. He declares his love to Isabel. Although she has been expecting this, at least in her imagination, she is troubled by this threat to her liberty, and she asks him to leave. Osmond agrees but, before leaving, he casually asks her to visit his daughter in Florence. The request is significant because it reveals his selfish and manipulative character as he uses his innocent daughter to achieve his ends.

When Isabel visits Pansy a few days later (**chapter thirty**), she is struck by the girl's innocence and her devotion to her father. Pansy quickly feels deep affection for Isabel and asks when she will return. Isabel tells her it will not be for a long time, to which the child responds, "I am only a little girl, . . . but I shall always expect you."

In **chapter thirty-one**, a year has passed, and Isabel is at the window of Mrs. Touchett's home in Florence, waiting for a visitor. Flashbacks of how she spent the past year serve more to expand the scope of Isabel's experience for the reader than to probe her mind. She is ready to make decisions. The first such decision is to reject firmly and finally the marriage proposal of Caspar Goodwood (**chapter thirty-two**). Although Caspar attracts Isabel more strongly than any other character in the novel, her rejection of him may also be seen as a rejection of her American past. Mrs. Touchett is not pleased with Isabel's choice of Gilbert Osmond, whom she refers to as Madame Merle's "friend," much to Isabel's annoyance (**chapter thirty-three**). When Mrs. Touchett tells Ralph of Isabel's intentions, he is "shocked and humiliated; his calculations had been false, and his cousin was lost. . . . He felt cold about the heart; he had never liked anything less." Isabel rents a carriage early each morning and drives into the woods to meet and walk with Osmond.

Ralph arrives in Florence, obviously ill, and Isabel fears that he may not live long (**chapter thirty-three**). Isabel finds him in the garden after returning from her drive one morning (**chapter thirty-four**). Ralph tells her he is thinking of her engagement to Osmond and how marriage to such a man will put her in a cage. He is struck by her conviction of the truth of her delusions as she replies that, unlike the more socially impressive Lord Warburton, Gilbert Osmond has "no property, no title, no honours, no houses, nor lands, nor position, nor reputation, nor brilliant belongings of any sort. It is the total absence of all these things that pleases me. Mr. Osmond is simply a man—he is not a proprietor." How egalitarian. How American. Ralph can do nothing to dissuade her. She will decide for herself.

Chapter thirty-five marks the end of the second section of the novel, relating Isabel's choice and how she arrives at it. Osmond assesses that Isabel is "present of incalculable value" from Madame Merle. The scene is juxtaposed, in **chapter thirty-six**, with a shift to a time when, almost four years later, Edward (Ned) Rosier (another American in Europe, introduced in **chapter twenty**) has fallen in love with Pansy Osmond. In this chapter we learn several things about the marriage between Isabel and Gilbert Osmond: Madame Merle, not Isabel, interviews the prospective bridegroom, determining that his income is inadequate for all but a modest life; Isabel has money and her husband does not, although he appears to be a rich man; Isabel had a son who died at six months. Somewhat mysteriously, Madame Merle advises Ned not to approach Mrs. Osmond whom, he thinks, will support his proposal to Pansy: "[D]on't for the present try to make her take up the cudgels for you," she tells him. "Her husband may have other views, and, as a person who wishes her well, I advise you not to multiply the points of difference between them." The consequences of Isabel's choice and the character of Gilbert Osmond will shape the third section of the novel in chapters thirty-six through fifty-two.

In **chapter thirty-seven**, Ned Rosier hopes to talk with Mrs. Osmond on a Thursday evening, the time Isabel customarily reserves for visitors and close friends. We see Isabel and the company through his eyes: "The years had touched her only to enrich her; the flower of her youth had not faded, it only hung more quietly on its stem. She had lost something of that quick eagerness to which her husband had privately taken exception—she had more the air of being able to wait . . . [She was] the picture of a gracious lady." Osmond, obviously informed of the young man's intentions by Madame Merle, is rude and embarrasses Ned. Ned has promised Madame Merle that he will not speak to Pansy this evening, but, when Madame Merle sees Pansy leave a room and Ned following her, she insists that he come to see her the next day at quarter past five. He applies to Isabel for some help amidst what he finds to be intolerable treatment; Isabel declines, telling him that she can do nothing.

When Ned visits Madame Merle the next day (**chapter thirty-eight**) he is surprised by her kindness to him. She advises only that he visit Pansy less and avoid Mr. Osmond, if at all possible. The next Thursday evening Ned confronts Osmond, who tells him that he is not a suitable match for Pansy. Ned tries to stand firm, but Osmond is distracted by the arrival of Lord Warburton, who has accompanied Ralph to Rome. Osmond remembers Warburton from the encounter in Rome four years earlier. Osmond leaves Isabel and Warburton alone, and Warburton tells her that Ralph is dying; she immediately says that she will go to see him. Warburton asks her if she is happy, and she assures him that she is. They both look across the room at Pansy; he remarks on her beauty, she that the girl is Osmond's daughter.

Ralph Touchett sees clearly the character of Gilbert Osmond and the effect of this marriage upon Isabel. His devotion to his cousin's happiness is what has kept him alive. Isabel visits Ralph several times, and he tells Warburton that he will remain in Rome rather than move to the warmer climate of Sicily. This decision will cost him his life, and Warburton is concerned. Ralph suggests that Warburton marry Pansy Osmond, that her father will be pleased to match her with an English nobleman. Warburton becomes angry when Ralph reminds him that marriage to Pansy will bring him near to Isabel.

In **chapter forty**, Isabel's sense that there is a strange intimacy between her husband and Madame Merle is confirmed. In a subtle scene in which the two engage in a quiet and intense conversation, James reveals their closeness through Isabel's eyes. When her husband and Madame Merle both argue that she must help to seal the union between Pansy and Warburton, she notes how similar their arguments are, how united their interests seem to be. Osmond meets alone with Isabel in **chapter forty-one** to convince her that she must exert her influence upon Pansy to accept Warburton. After Osmond leaves, in **chapter forty-two**, Isabel realizes that she does not trust either her husband or Madame Merle. She has been mistaken: "She had taken all the first steps in the purest confidence, and then she had suddenly found the infinite vista of a multiplied life to be a dark, narrow alley, with a dead wall at the end. . . . [S]he simply believed that he hated her." She begins to reflect upon the decisions she has made.

Three nights later, Isabel and Pansy attend a party without Osmond (**chapter forty-three**). Ned Rosier is also there, and, while Pansy is dancing, he approaches Isabel to ask about Pansy. Isabel offers no encouragement, and the young man leaves as Pansy returns to Isabel's side. While Pansy is again dancing, Warburton confirms to Isabel that he has written the letter to Osmond asking for Pansy's hand but has not yet sent it. She leaves Warburton to tell Rosier that she will now help him. He is understandably surprised. As she leaves the party, she reminds Warburton to send the letter. Nothing is clear; she must have a plan. In **chapter forty-four**, Henrietta Stackpole pays an unexpected visit to the Countess Gemini to inquire about Isabel. The Countess is reluctant to speak with her, but Henrietta is disturbed by the woman's references to Lord Warburton's visits to the Osmonds. She suspects that her friend is unhappy. She calls Caspar Goodwood and convinces him to accompany her to see Isabel.

In **chapter forty-five**, Isabel realizes that Lord Warburton is still in love with her and not with Pansy. Although her actions will make her life with Osmond more difficult, she will not allow Pansy to suffer in a loveless marriage. She tells the girl that her father has forbidden a marriage with Ned Rosier; he wants her to marry someone with more money. She mentions Lord Warburton, and Pansy is relieved because she knows that he does not love her and will never actually marry her. An engagement to Warburton, however, would protect her from other offers and shelter her love for Rosier. Isabel is impressed with her rational mind.

Chapter forty-six further marks the contrast between Osmond's despicable character and Isabel's essential integrity. When Warburton's letter fails to arrive as expected, Osmond accuses Isabel of working against him, of intercepting the letter herself. Warburton arrives to announce that he has been recalled and must return to England, leaving Ralph in Rome. Isabel's deep disappointment in her husband is linked to her thoughts about Madame Merle as she wonders if the woman is friend or foe (**chapter forty-seven**). In waking dreams, Isabel dimly envisions the intimacy of the relationship between Madame Merle and Osmond. When Madame Merle discovers that Warburton will not be marrying Pansy, she asks Isabel, with contempt, "What on earth did you do with Lord Warburton?" and Isabel thinks, "As if it were any business of hers!"

Ralph Touchett decides to leave Rome and return to England in **chapter forty-eight**, in order that he may die at home. To Ralph's amusement, Henrietta, all efficiency and goodwill, offers to accompany him home and care for him there; Caspar Goodwood makes a similar offer, because Isabel had asked it of him. Henrietta advises Isabel to leave Osmond before the marriage changes her. Isabel visits Ralph and tells him that she would like to accompany him home, but both know the difficulty it would cause with her husband. She tells him that she will come if he sends for her. They both know that this will only be on his deathbed. "I shall keep that for my last pleasure," he tells her.

Madame Merle visits Isabel in **chapter forty-nine**. She asks Isabel to explain her exact role in Warburton's decision and departure. Isabel realizes, with horror, that she has underestimated Madame Merle all along: "Who are you—what are you? . . . What have you done with my husband? . . . What have you done with me?" she asks, to which Madame Merle answers, "Everything!" Isabel realizes that her marriage to Osmond had not been her own choice, after all. That choice had been arranged by Madame Merle. But Madame Merle, too, has been duped by Osmond. She confronts him, denouncing her own participation in their manipulation of Isabel; Osmond is indifferent to her criticism.

In **chapter fifty**, Ned Rosier tells Isabel that he has sold his possessions and has fifty thousand dollars to bring to a marriage with Pansy. Will Mr. Osmond now accept him, he wants to know. Isabel offers only that he deserves to succeed but that Osmond still intends for his daughter to marry a nobleman. A week later, Pansy announces to Isabel that, because Osmond wishes it, she will return to the convent; within half an hour she departs. At dinner, the Countess Gemini mentions her own affection for Rosier, and Osmond threatens to banish her from his household if she encourages the relationship between Pansy and Ned.

A telegram to Isabel from Mrs. Touchett announces that Ralph is dying (**chapter fifty-one**). He wants to see Isabel. She immediately tells Osmond that she will go to Gardencourt. This confrontation between the couple is the climax of the third part of the novel, the point at which Isabel makes her most adult and clear-eyed decision. Osmond is revealed as the selfish cad he is and Isabel as the decisive and responsible woman she has become. The Countess Gemini finally reveals to Isabel the true nature of Osmond's relations with Madame Merle, that Pansy is their daughter. Upon hearing this, Isabel feels pity for Madame Merle, a reaction that astonishes the Countess.

Before Isabel boards the train to Paris, she decides to visit Pansy at the convent (**chapter fifty-two**). Madame Merle is already there, and she quickly realizes that Isabel has learned the truth. Madame Merle waits as Isabel visits Pansy, alone. Pansy is sad that Isabel must leave for England, but she makes her stepmother promise to return. Isabel replies, "I won't desert you." From Madame Merle Isabel learns that the inheritance from Daniel Touchett was arranged by Ralph. Isabel tells her that she never wants to see her again. Many matters are settled in this chapter: Isabel gains knowledge and decides to defy Osmond; the character of Madame Merle is fully revealed; and Isabel maintains her commitment to Pansy, thereby protecting the young girl from manipulation and unhappiness.

Isabel arrives in London in **chapter fifty-three**, and is met by Henrietta Stackpole. Isabel is amused to learn that her friend, a fierce critic of all things English, is engaged to marry an Englishman. Although Isabel wants to see Ralph immediately, Henrietta convinces her to rest in London that evening. The next day Isabel arrives at Gardencourt (**chapter fifty-four**), and Mrs. Touchett tells her that Ralph has been sleeping most of the day. At dinner that evening, Mrs. Touchett tells her niece that Lord Warburton will soon be married and asks if she has ever regretted rejecting Warburton's proposal. Isabel is pleased for Warburton and expresses no regrets. After dinner she goes to see Ralph. He does not speak but is aware of her presence. Three days later, he is able to converse with his cousin, and they share their affections and their mutual understanding. He tells Isabel to "[R]emember this, that if you have been hated, you have also been loved." Isabel replies, "Ah, my brother!" and concludes the final union of the novel's most intelligent and sensitive characters.

In the final chapter of *The Portrait of a Lady* (**chapter fifty-five**), Ralph is dead, and Isabel returns to Gilbert Osmond, a move that has confounded readers and critics. But her promise to Pansy will be fulfilled, and Isabel will remain true to her character. ✣

—Tenley Williams
New York University

List of Characters

Isabel Archer is a twenty-three-year-old American brought to England by her Aunt Lydia Touchett in order to broaden her experience. Isabel is a free spirit, determined to make her own decisions. Her weakness is that she sees people and events as she imagines them to be, not as they are. Her most idealistic belief is that she can make a free choice. As the novel progresses, the choices Isabel makes reveal her constancy, courage, nobility, and imagination. *The Portrait of a Lady* is the portrait of Isabel.

Mrs. Lydia Touchett is Isabel's aunt and Ralph's mother. She is an eccentric and seemingly independent woman, an American in Europe who carefully observes the restraints and demands of European decorum. She brings Isabel to England because she sees in her niece the potential for intellectual growth.

Mr. Daniel Touchett is the father of Ralph. A wealthy, retired American banker, he has been in England many years. When Lydia brings Isabel home to Gardencourt, both he and Ralph respond to her personality and charm. He and Isabel develop an important friendship that leads him, at the urging of his son, to provide her with a substantial inheritance upon his death.

Ralph Touchett is Isabel's cousin. He is the most perceptive of the characters in the novel and the one who best understands Isabel. Although he seems detached from physical and emotional passions because of his debilitating illness, his condition allows him to observe the characters clearly; he sees through all artifice. Ralph lives through his cousin, Isabel, and he does all he can to help her to fulfill her hopes in life.

Lord Warburton is an English nobleman in love with Isabel. Although Isabel rejects him, his love for her remains constant. Gilbert Osmond hopes he will marry Pansy, but Warburton's noble character prevails and he resists Osmond's manipulation.

Caspar Goodwood is Isabel's American suitor. The two had met before Mrs. Touchett invited Isabel to come to England. Caspar is aggressive and persistent in his pursuit of Isabel, but she rejects him both at the beginning of the novel and at the end, before she returns to Gilbert Osmond.

Henrietta Stackpole is a brash and independent young journalist and Isabel's constant friend. She is the picture of the American in Europe, defending American habits against European stuffiness. Isabel thinks Henrietta to be an example of the ideal, American, professional woman who leads a successful and useful life.

Madame Merle at first represents, for Isabel, the ideal European personality. She is controlled, cultured, socially respected, and worldly. Isabel is horrified to learn that Pansy is the daughter of Madame Merle and Gilbert Osmond. Madame Merle has manipulated events only to advance her child's interests and, in the end, Isabel pities her.

Gilbert Osmond is an attractive and urbane man whom Isabel marries. He is the villain of the story, the character whose selfishness and evil are seen most clearly by Ralph Touchett. He uses Isabel's wealth, Madame Merle, and even Pansy, for his own ends.

Pansy Osmond is the young daughter of Madame Merle and Gilbert Osmond. She is convent educated, innocent, and has great admiration for Isabel. Isabel decides to return to her husband at the novel's end in order to save Pansy from his manipulation and greed.

Edward (Ned) Rosier is another American in Europe, a childhood friend of Isabel's who falls in love with Pansy Osmond.

Countess Gemini is Gilbert Osmond's sister. She is much more perceptive than her apparent shallowness indicates to the other characters, including Ralph Touchett. Out of concern for Isabel's fate, she reveals to Isabel the truth of the relationship between Gilbert Osmond and Madame Merle. ✤

Critical Views

JOHN HAY ON CHARACTER DELINEATION IN *THE PORTRAIT OF A LADY*

[John Hay (1838–1905) was an American statesman, poet, and historian. He contributed to many periodicals of his day and reviewed books regularly for the *New York Tribune*. He is also the author of the acclaimed *Abraham Lincoln: A History* (1890). In this early review of *The Portrait of a Lady*, Hay examines the criticism that the "portrait" of Isabel Archer is one of the least clearly delineated in James's novel.]

If there is anything in the motto of "art for art's sake," if the way of doing a thing is, as many claim, of more importance in literature than the thing done, then this last novel of Mr. James needs no justification or apology. No work printed in recent years, on either side [of] the Atlantic or on either side [of] the English Channel, surpasses this in seriousness of intention, in easy scope and mastery of material, in sustained and spontaneous dignity and grace of style, in wit and epigram, and, on the whole, in clear conception and accurate delineation of character. The title was a stumbling-block to many, as the story pursued its leisurely course in *The Atlantic Monthly*, and now that it is finished it is the title which affords to criticism its easiest attack. It is claimed that the heroine is of all the characters the one least clearly painted, least perfectly understood. But it would not be difficult to say that we know as much of her and of her motives as the author chooses for us to know, and the interest of the novel comes in great part from the vagueness of our acquaintance with Miss Archer; and after all, when we lay down the book, we cannot deny, if we are candid, that we know as much of the motives which induced her to refuse two gallant gentlemen and to marry a selfish and soulless scoundrel as we do of the impulses which lead our sisters and cousins to similar results. No one can complain of the clearness with which the other characters are drawn. There is hardly a sharper portrait in our literature, and certainly none more delightful, than Ralph Touchett. None who read the opening chapters of the story a year ago can forget the slight shiver of apprehension they felt when Mr. James distinctly announced that Ralph Touchett was clever, and when Lord Warburton declared that "he was never bored when he came to Gardencourt; one gets such uncommonly good talk." It shows a fine arrogance in the most hardened jouster to throw such a challenge as that. It is said that Shakespeare killed Mercutio early in the play where he appears [*Romeo and Juliet*], for fear of being killed by him; but Mr. James evidently has no such fear of his own creations: From the first chapter to the last, Ralph is "clever, witty and charming," as Mr. James tells us in the beginning, with a charm which overcomes the tedium of hopeless illness and the repulsiveness of death. The book is full of living and breathing characters. Mr. Trollope has never drawn a better English nobleman than Lord Warburton, the splendor of whose environment is delicately suggested, never described, and whose manners are painted in a dozen subtle phrases like these: "He had a certain fortunate, brilliant, exceptional look—the air of a happy temperament fertilized by a high civilization—which would have made almost any observer envy him at a venture"; "his English address, in which a vague shyness seemed to offer itself as an element of good breeding; in which the only defect was a difficulty of achieving transitions." The portrait of Osmond is one of those wonderful pictures in which Mr. James excels, drawn entirely from the outside, but as perfect as if his acts and conversations had been supplemented by voluminous pages of soliloquy. His sister the Countess is equally good; so is the dry, practical, caustic Mrs. Touchett; so is the travelling newspaper woman, Miss Stackpole.

—John Hay, "James's *The Portrait of a Lady* (1881)," *The Merrill Studies in The Portrait of a Lady*, ed. Lyall H. Powers (Columbus, OH: Charles E. Merrill Publishing, 1970), pp. 1–2.

✤

Joseph Warren Beach on Henry James's Narrative Method

[Joseph Warren Beach (1880–1957) was a prominent critic and literary historian. He is the author of *The Concept of Nature in Nineteenth-Century English Poetry* (1936) and *American Fiction, 1920–1940* (1941). In the following extract, taken from *The Method of Henry James* (1918), Beach discusses James's method of revealing his portrait of Isabel Archer and filling in the background characters.]

Essentially "The Portrait" is the development of an idea by the method of "revelation" described in our first part. The adventures of Isabel Archer are more spiritual than material. The stages of her chronicle are the stages by which the painter fills out her portrait. Even in the preliminary period of her English sojourn, we are occupied with the discovery of a woman intensely concerned to make her life fine, hoping "to find herself in a difficult position, so that she should have the pleasure of being as heroic as the occasion demanded." The proposal of Lord Warburton is admitted merely in order that she may assert in striking fashion her "enlightened prejudice in favour of the free exploration of life." It is not ease and security that are desired by this adventurous American soul. She explains to her reproachful suitor that she cannot hope to escape her fate, cannot avoid unhappiness by separating herself from life—"from the usual chances and dangers, from what most people know and suffer."

With the entry of Madame Merle towards the end of the first volume, the painter attacks the real background of his picture. A few chapters later his task begins in earnest with the appearance of the Florentine gentleman who is to become the most prominent feature in the heroine's experience. From this point on, the work is a masterpiece of revelation; and if the details brought out are chiefly details of "background"—having to do with the characters of Osmond and Madame Merle—that is essentially the case in the later books. The background circumstances are revealed through the consciousness of the heroine who is the foreground figure; and they tend to bring out in brighter relief the beauty of this figure. Every trait of vanity and selfishness in Osmond gives play to the corresponding traits of generous large-mindedness in Isabel, as well as giving her occasion for the display of resourcefulness in difficult social relations. The coldness of his nature serves as foil to the flame-like warmth of hers. And the earlier stages of their acquaintance bring out sufficiently the large ground of taste and sensibility which they have in common. I must deny myself the agreeable task of tracing from scene to scene the nicely graduated steps by which this "sterile dilettante" is betrayed to us first and then to Isabel, and the steps by which there dawn upon her consciousness the more and more bewildering, the more and more heroic features of her great adventure.

Nowhere is the concern of the story more beautifully than in "The Portrait" the *quality* of experience. It is not the bare facts of Gilbert's relation to Madame Merle and Pansy, revealed at the climax of the story by the Countess Gemini, that are of importance. It is the values of life as conceived by Gilbert and by Madame Merle upon which these facts throw their final interpretive light. Nowhere is there a finer indication of those social and aesthetic values to which all the leading characters of James are devoted than in the scenes of Isabel's growing admiration for Osmond. Nowhere short of "Poynton" and "The Golden Bowl" is there a finer display of the spiritual values that transcend the others than in the scenes of Isabel's growing horror of her husband. "The Portrait of a Lady" has thus the distinction of being the first novel in which the "figure in the carpet" stands out in distinct and glowing beauty.

—Joseph Warren Beach, "Henry James' Narrative Method," *The Method of Henry James* (Philadelphia: Albert Saifer, 1954). pp. 208–10.

✤

GRAHAM GREENE ON ARCHITECTURAL IMAGERY IN *THE PORTRAIT OF A LADY*

[Graham Greene (1904–1991), the celebrated English novelist, was also a journalist, travel writer, playwright, and a regular book reviewer. He was, for a time, literary editor on the *Spectator* and *Night and Day*. In the following introduction to the 1947 edition of *The Portrait of a Lady*, Greene looks at the architectural imagery presented in the novel and places it in the context of other works by James.]

"The conception of a certain young lady affronting her destiny"—that is how Henry James described the subject of this book, for which he felt, next to *The Ambassadors*, the greatest personal tenderness. In his wonderful preface (for no other book in the collected edition of his works did he write a preface so rich in revelations and memories) he compares *The Portrait of a Lady* several times to a building, and it is as a great, leisurely built cathedral that one thinks of it, with immense smooth pillars, side-chapels, and aisles, and a dark crypt where Ralph Touchett lies in marble like a crusader with his feet crossed to show that he has seen the Holy Land; sometimes, indeed, it may seem to us too ample a shrine for one portrait until we remember that this master-craftsman always has his reasons: those huge pillars are required to bear the weight of Time (that dark backward and abysm that is the novelist's abiding problem): the succession of side-chapels are all designed to cast their particular light upon the high altar: no vista is without its ambiguous purpose. The whole building, indeed, is a triumph of architectural planning: the prentice hand which had already produced some works—*Roderick Hudson* and *The American*—impressive if clumsy, and others—*The Europeans* and *Washington Square*—graceful if slight, had at last learnt the whole secret of planning for permanence. And the subject? "A certain young woman affronting her destiny." Does it perhaps still, at first thought, seem a little inadequate?

The answer, of course, is that it all depends on the destiny, and about the destiny Henry James has in his preface nothing to tell us. He is always something of a conjurer in these prefaces: he seems ready to disclose everything—the source of his story: the technique of its writing: even the room in which he settles down to work and the noises of the street outside. Sometimes he blinds the reader with a bold sleight of hand, calling, for example, *The Turn of the Screw* "a fairy-tale pure and simple." We must always remain on guard while reading these prefaces, for at a certain level no writer has really disclosed less.

The plot in the case of this novel is far from being an original one: it is as if James, looking round for the events which were to bring his young woman, Isabel Archer, into play, had taken the first at hand: a fortune-hunter, the fortune-hunter's unscrupulous mistress, and a young American heiress caught in the meshes of a loveless marriage. (He was to use almost identically the same plot but with deeper implications and more elaborate undertones in *The Wings of the Dove*.) We can almost see the young James laying down some popular three-decker of the period in his Roman or Venetian lodging and wondering, "What could I do with even that story?" For a plot after all is only the machinery—the machinery which will show the young woman (what young woman?) affronting her destiny (but what destiny?). In his preface, apparently so revealing, James has no answer to these questions. Nor is there anything there which will help us to guess what element it was in the melodramatic plot that attracted the young writer at this moment when he came first into his full powers as a novelist, and again years later when as an old man he set to work to crown his career with the three poetic masterpieces *The Wings of the Dove*, *The Ambassadors*, and *The Golden Bowl*.

—Graham Greene, Introduction to *The Portrait of a Lady* by Henry James (London: Oxford University Press, 1947). pp. v–vi.

F. R. LEAVIS ON MADAME MERLE, THE COUNTESS GEMINI, AND PANSY

[F. R. Leavis (1895–1978) was the founder of an influential school of criticism, known as New Criticism, at Cambridge University, where he lectured for many years. He authored *Fiction and the Reading Public* (1932), a study of the relationship between literature and literacy, and *The Great Tradition* (1948), which traces the history of the British novel. He was also the founder and chief editor of the quarterly *Scrutiny*. In the following extract, taken from *The Great Tradition*, he praises the richness of James's novel and examines the characters Madame Merle, Countess Gemini, and Pansy.]

[The novel's] greatness derives from [James's] peculiar genius and experience, and it embodies an organization of his vital interests. These interests inform everything in it: the wit, the dialogue, the plot, the characterization.

The creative wealth of the book is all distinctively Jamesian. Madame Merle, for instance, couldn't have been done by George Eliot. The vision here is Isabel's, who hasn't yet seen through her:

> She had become too flexible, too useful, was too ripe and too final. She was in a word too perfectly the social animal that man and woman are supposed to have been intended to be; and she had rid herself of every remnant of that tonic wildness which we may assume to have belonged even to the most amiable persons in the ages before country-house life was the fashion. Isabel found it difficult to think of her in any detachment or privacy, she existed only in her relations, direct or indirect, with her fellow-mortals. One might wonder what commerce she could possibly hold with her own spirit. One always ended, however, by feeling that a charming surface doesn't necessarily prove one superficial; this was an illusion in which, in one's youth, one had but just escaped being nourished. Madame Merle was not superficial—not she. She was deep. . . .

She represents, that is, a social "civilization" ("the great round world itself") that is not of the kind James himself is after (just as she is, with Osmond, the complete expatriate who has none of the American virtues). The contrasting Mrs. Touchett reminds us of an American type we meet in some of Lawrence's best work (*St. Mawr*, for instance). James presents her with his characteristic wit—which, as I have said, is no mere surface-habit of expression: "The edges of her conduct were so very clear-cut that for susceptible persons it sometimes had a knife-like effect." Henrietta Stackpole is another American type, perfectly done—marvelously escaping the effect of caricature, and remaining for all her portentous representativeness, sufficiently sympathetic. Then there is Osmond's sister, the Countess Gemini, "a lady who had so mismanaged her improprieties that they had ceased to hang together at all . . . and had become the mere floating fragments of a wrecked renown, incommoding social circulation," and who would plunge into a lucid conversation "as a poodle plunges after a thrown stick."

The Countess Gemini, though so well done, is a weakness in the book, in the sense that she is too simply there to serve as a piece of machinery. She alone can reveal to Isabel the clandestine relations of Osmond and Madame Merle, and the fact that Pansy is their daughter, and she is given no sufficient motives for performing the service. Pansy herself raises the question of James's attitude toward the pure protected *jeune fille* (the "blank page"), a type to which he seems curiously drawn. In *The Awkward Age* he shows the good little Aggie, the foil to Nanda, developing after her marriage into something approaching, at the level of Edwardian smart society, a vulgar trollop: and we readily accept the implication that, in such a milieu, the development follows naturally out of such "innocence." In *The Ambassadors* he seems to confirm this implication by giving the decidedly not innocent Madame Vionnet another carefully guarded "blank page" for daughter.

Though Pansy serves obvious functions as machinery in the relations between Isabel and Osmond, her presence in the book has, in addition, some point. As a representative figure, "the white flower of cultivated sweetness," she pairs in contrast with Henrietta Stackpole, the embodiment of a quite different innocence—a robust American innocence that thrives on free exposure to the world. She brings us, in fact, to the general observation that almost all the characters can be seen to have, in the same way, their values and significances in a total scheme. For though *The Portrait of a Lady* is on so much of a larger scale than *The Europeans*, and because of its complexity doesn't invite the description of "moral fable," it is similarly organized: it is all intensely significant. It offers no largesse of irrelevant "life;" its vitality is wholly that of art.

—F. R. Leavis, *The Great Tradition: George Eliot, Henry James, Joseph Conrad* (London: Chatto & Windus, 1948), pp. 150–52.

✤

Dorothy Van Ghent on James's Americans Abroad

[Dorothy Van Ghent was a prolific critic and biographer. She is the author of *Keats: the Myth of the Hero* (1983) and *Willa Cather* (1964). In the following extract, taken from Van Ghent's most celebrated work, *The English Novel: Form and Function* (1953), she examines the "international myth" of a vibrant, new America searching for culture and history in the Old World.]

The "international myth" that operates broadly in James's work, and that appears, in this novel, in the typical confrontation of American innocence and moral rigor with the tortuosities of an older civilization, gives its own and special dimension to the moneyed prospect. James came to maturity in a post-Civil War America euphoric with material achievement. In terms of the Jamesian "myth," American wealth is now able to buy up the whole museum of Europe, all its visible "point" of art objects and culture prestige, to take back home and set up in the front yard (we need look no further, for historical objectification of this aspect of the "myth," than to William Randolph Hearst's epic importation of various priceless chunks of Europe to California). If the shadows of the physically dispossessed—the sweat and bone-weariness and the manifold anonymous deprivation in which this culture-buying power had its source—are excluded from James's money-gilded canvas, the shadow of spiritual dispossession is the somber shape under the money outline. We are not allowed to forget the aesthetic and moral impoverishment that spread its gross vacuum at the core of the American acquisitive dream—the greed, the obtuse or rapacious presumption, the disvaluation of values that kept pace to pace with material expansion. James's characteristic thematic contrasts, here as in other novels, are those of surface against depth, inspection against experience, buying power against living power, the American tourist's cultural balcony against the European abyss of history and memory and involved motive where he perilously or callously teeters. In *The Portrait*, the American heroine's pilgrimage in Europe becomes a fatally serious spiritual investment, an investment of the "free" self in and with the circumstantial and binding past, a discovery of the relations of the self with history, and a moral renovation of history in the freedom of the individual conscience. It is a growing of more delicate and deeper-reaching roots and a nourishment of a more complex, more troubled, more creatively personal humanity. It is, in short, what is ideally meant by "civilization," as that word refers to a process that can take place within an individual.

The postulate of wealth and privilege is, in revised terms, that of the second chapter of Genesis (the story of Adam in the garden)—that of the optimum conditions which will leave the innocent soul at liberty to develop its own potentialities—and, as in the archetype of the Fall of Man, the postulate is significant not as excluding knowledge of good and evil, but as presenting a rare opportunity for such knowledge. It is the bounty poured on Isabel Archer (significantly, the man who gives her the symbolical investiture of money is a man who is fatally ill; significantly, also, she is under an illusion as to the giver) that makes her "free" to determine her choice of action, and thus morally most responsible for her choice; but it is the very bounty of her fortune, also, that activates at once, as if chemically, the proclivity to evil in the world of privilege that her wealth allows her to enter—it is her money that draws Madame Merle and Osmond to her; so that her "freedom" is actualized as imprisonment, in a peculiarly ashen and claustral, because peculiarly refined, suburb of hell. Isabel's quest had, at the earliest, been a quest for happiness—the naively egotistic American quest; it converts into a problem of spiritual salvation, that is, into a quest of "life;" and again the Biblical archetype shadows forth the problem. After eating of the fruit of the tree of knowledge of good and evil, how is one to regain access to the tree of life? ⟨. . .⟩

The Portrait identifies life with the most probing, dangerous, responsible awareness—identifies, as it were, the two "trees," the tree of the Fall and the tree of the Resurrection. The heroine's voluntary search for fuller consciousness leads her, in an illusion of perfect freedom to choose only "the best" in experience, to choose an evil; but it is this that, by providing insight through suffering and guilt, provides also access to life—to the fructification of consciousness that is a knowledge of human bondedness.

—Dorothy Van Ghent, *The English Novel: Form and Function* (New York: Rinehart & Co., 1953), pp. 213–14, 215.

Richard Poirier on Narration and Diction in *The Portrait of a Lady*

[Richard Poirier is the Director of Graduate Studies and the Marius Bewley Professor of American and English Literature at Rutgers University and the founder and editor of *Raritan: A Quarterly Review*. He is the author of *Norman Mailer* (1972) and *Poetry and Pragmatism* (1992). In this excerpt from *The Comic Sense of Henry James: A Study of the Early Novels* (1960), Poirier comments on the aristocratic detachment of James's narrator in *The Portrait of a Lady*.]

The style through which James expresses his role as the observer and narrator in *The Portrait of the Lady* is an indication of his security, of the achieved aristocracy of his position. This is particularly apparent in the quality of the comedy, where there is represented that ideally civilized view of experience which Isabel desires and which she fails to detect in

Ralph. James's style has the characteristics, put into language, which identify Ralph as the most admirably intelligent character in the novel. He has, we are told, an inclination to "jocosity and irony," a phrase which James significantly changes in the revision to "adventure and irony." The latter words aptly describe the nature of the comedy in this novel—it is used to champion the cause of speculativeness and imagination and to expose the various seductions to which it may fall prey. James's tone, and, by his leave, Ralph's, is affectionate and encouraging, but it is also superior; it is tolerant, but it is above all self-confident. By the moderation of voice in the narrative style, particularly in the first half when Isabel is being introduced, James constrains us to habits of response and understanding that make us sympathetic observers of Isabel's career and partisans of the values to which she subscribes.

While James's voice at the opening is not identical with Ralph's, it expresses an equally amused and undefensive urbanity of mind. For a good half of the passage with which the novel begins, the tone has a quality which is characteristic of certain observable features of English conversation. There is a noticeable habit of verbal exaggeration, by which relatively small things assume extraordinary proportions, accompanied by extremely imposing discriminations about them. The total effect is close to the mock epic. The first paragraph sounds as if James were sifting the afternoon into exquisite little pieces, giving the whole description a kind of elegant prissiness:

> Under certain circumstances there are few hours in life more agreeable than the hour dedicated to the ceremony known as afternoon tea. There are circumstances in which, whether you partake of the tea or not—some people of course never do—the situation is in itself delightful. These that I have in mind in beginning to unfold this simple history offered an admirable setting to an innocent pastime. The implements of the little feast had been disposed upon the lawn of an old English country-house, in what I should call the perfect middle of a splendid summer afternoon. Part of the afternoon had waned, but much of it was left, and what was left was of the finest and rarest quality. Real dusk would not arrive for many hours; but the flood of summer light had begun to ebb, the air had grown mellow, the shadows were long upon the smooth, dense turf. They lengthened slowly, however, and the scene expressed that

sense of leisure still to come which is perhaps the chief source of one's enjoyment of such a scene at such an hour. From five o'clock to eight is on certain occasions a little eternity; but on such an occasion as this the interval could be only an eternity of pleasure.

The diction, none of which was altered in the revision, has a fastidious pomposity—"ceremony known as afternoon tea," "some people of course never do"—and we are to imagine this use of language not as part of an impersonal narration, but as a fairly personal address—note the use of "I"—from someone striking a very individual social posture. The fastidiousness and the pomposity are harmlessly and, therefore, the more amusingly expended upon an event which is by no means less delightful than he claims. But his eager discriminations, the minute measurement of the remnants of the afternoon, the repetitions of words like "such" and "certain," give an excessive and correspondingly satiric note to the ritualized feelings that are at the same time being commended. James assumes a definable role in this passage. He sounds like an overly impressed American who has "gone" English, who is more English than the English. None the less, the voice teases itself, as of a man who does take delight in English habits, but with such amused and self-assured adaptability that he can exaggerate and gently spoof them.

—Richard Poirier, *The Comic Sense of Henry James: A Study of the Early Novels* (New York: Oxford University Press, 1960), pp. 190–92.

✤

Leon Edel on Some Possible Models for Isabel Archer from James's Life

[Leon Edel, Professor Emeritus of New York University, was an important Henry James scholar. Among his many works are *James Joyce: The Last Journey* (1947) and *Bloomsbury: A House of Lions* (1979), a much acclaimed study of England's Bloomsbury writers. In the following extract, taken from *Henry James. The Conquest of London: 1870–1881* (1962), Edel traces some possible real-life models for Isabel Archer.]

The Portrait of a Lady was the third of Henry James's large studies of the American abroad and twice as long as either of its predecessors. In *Roderick Hudson* he had posed the case of the artist, the limitations of his American background, and the frustration of his creative energy from the moment it was confronted by passion. In *The American* he had pictured an ambitious businessman, bent on civilizing himself, proud enough to know his worth, and arrogant enough to think that the best of Europe was none too good for him. *The Portrait* was envisaged as a kind of feminine version of *The American*, and James began with the thought that his Isabel Archer would be a female Christopher Newman. Indeed this may be why he named her Isabel; there is a certain logic in moving from Christopher to the Queen who sent him faring across the ocean. And Isabel Archer deems herself good enough to be a queen; she embodies a notion not unlike that of Isabella of Boston, whose motto was *C'est mon plaisir*.

In Isabel Archer, Henry wished to draw "the character and aspect of a particularly engaging young woman," and to show her in the act of "affronting her destiny." Like her male predecessors she goes abroad a thorough provincial, with her "meagre knowledge, her inflated ideals, her confidence at once innocent and dogmatic, her temper at once exacting and indulgent." A person who is dogmatic and exacting on the strength of meagre knowledge can only be characterized as presumptuous; and there is presumption in Isabel, for all the delicacy of her feeling: presumption suggests also a strong measure of egotism. James presents her to us as a young romantic with high notions of what life will bring her; and also as one who tends to see herself in a strong dramatic light. She pays the penalty of giving "undue encouragement to the faculty of seeing without judging"; she takes things for granted on scanty evidence. The author confesses that she was "probably very liable to the sin of self-esteem; she often surveyed with complacency the field of her own nature." He speaks of her "mixture of curiosity and fastidiousness, of vivacity and indifference, her determination to see, to try, to know, her combination of the desultory flame-like spirit and the eager and personal creature of her conditions." And he adds: "She treated herself to occasions of homage."

The allusion to her "flame-like spirit" suggests that Isabel images Henry's long-dead cousin Minny Temple, for he was to describe her in the same way. He was to confess that he had actually thought of Minny, in creating the eager imagination and the intellectual shortcomings of his heroine. But Minny, as he pointed out to Grace Norton, had been "incomplete." Death had deprived her of the trials—and the joys—of maturity. Henry, as artist, could imagine and "complete" that which had been left undone. Nevertheless, if Isabel has something of Henry's cousin in her make-up, she has much of Henry himself. He endows her, at any rate, with the background of his own Albany childhood, and as in *Washington Square* he interpolates a section wholly autobiographical, depicting his grandmother's house, the Dutch school from which he himself had fled in rebellion (as Isabel does), the "capital peach trees," which he had always sampled and always remembered. The scene is re-evoked years later in the autobiographies.

The most Jamesian of Henry's heroines is thus closely linked by her background and her early life to her creator. And when Henry sends Isabel to Europe and makes her into an heiress, he places her in a predicament somewhat analogous to his own. Henry was hardly an "heir;" but his pen had won him a measure of the freedom which others possess through wealth. In posing the questions: what would Isabel do with her newfound privileges? where would she turn? how behave? he was seeking answers for himself as well as for her. The questions are asked in the novel by Ralph Touchett, Isabel's cousin, a sensitive invalid who has silently transferred his inheritance to her. He knows he has not long to live; and he wishes to see how Isabel's large nature will profit by endowment. If this is a sign of his love for her, and the sole way in which he can be symbolically united to her, it is also Ralph's way of living vicariously in Isabel's life and participating in whatever fate her temperament may reserve for her. He, too, has a substantial fund of egotism.

—Leon Edel, *Henry James 1870-1881: The Conquest of London* (Philadelphia: J.B. Lippincott, 1962), pp. 421–23.

✤

Walter F. Wright on Isabel Archer's Ancestors in James's Fiction

[Walter F. Wright is the Marie Kotouc Roberts Professor of English at the University of Nebraska and a literary critic. Among his publications are *Romance and Tragedy in Joseph Conrad* (1949) and *Art and Substance in George Meredith* (1953). Here, in a selection from *The Madness of Art: A Study of Henry James* (1962), Wright traces the development of Isabel Archer through James's earlier fiction.]

Isabel Archer is not without precursors in James's fiction. ⟨. . .⟩ Like the other American girls in James's works, Isabel is determined to maintain her liberty. Like them, she has a romantic idealization of Europe, and like some of them, she is a reader of literature. What we find in her portrait that gives it special significance is the patient care in the delineation of each feature. In *The Portrait of a Lady* there are a few awkward touches—an occasional self-conscious device in narration, resort two or three times to forced descriptions of Isabel's feelings, and a woodenness in some characterizations. But the reader, nevertheless, comes to feel that he has entered Isabel's mind and that he can appreciate her conflict and its resolution.

Isabel has lived much in her imagination, shaping her image of the world from her reading; she has even preferred to keep a door closed in order to imagine what lies beyond, and Henrietta Stackpole warns her that she lives "too much in the world of your own dreams." Isabel's life has been free from sorrow and unpleasantness. Indeed, she tells Ralph Touchett that "it's not absolutely necessary to suffer; we were not made for that." By her sensibility and her reading she is inclined toward a love of the past and a gentle, pensive appreciation of sadness removed from the immediate present. But she also possesses a willful illusion that life should be recklessly daring. When asked by Henrietta whether she knows where she is "drifting," she replies, "No, I haven't the least idea, and I find it very pleasant not to know. A swift carriage, of a dark night, rattling with four horses over roads that one can't see—that's my idea of happiness."

It is Isabel's own choices that introduce her unwittingly to sorrow and curtail the range in which choices can thereafter be made. Her decision to marry Osmond, she perceives, has brought sadness for Ralph, and her thoughts anticipate James's comments on the bliss and the bale: "It was the tragic part of happiness; one's right was always made of the wrong of someone else." From this time onward her experience in suffering widens rapidly; and though she has erred through ignorance, she insists on enduring the consequences. All sorts of choices have now been closed to her, but she holds to her freedom to choose. As she tells Henrietta, "one must accept one's deeds. . . . I was perfectly free [to marry or not marry Osmond]." She adds what has been implicit in her conduct: "It's not of him that I'm considerate—it's of myself!" Even after she has suffered humiliation and disillusionment she is still determined to seek no escape from responsibility; and though she cannot believe that it will be her fate to experience only suffering, she is resigned. That the price she pays is heavy is revealed in the last scenes. She must admit her love for the dying Ralph, and the admission reveals the bleak contrast between his world and her present married life. When kissed by the still-faithful Goodwood, she seems for a moment to float "in fathomless waters" before she regains mastery of herself and flees.

James remarks that she is "not a daughter of the Puritans." But in describing her independence in adversity, he writes,

"The old Protestant tradition had never faded from Isabel's imagination . . . ." In her zest for a full, even perilous adventure, Isabel is indeed not puritan, and though she has not found much cultural nourishment in Europe, she has avidly learned what she could of the Hellenic aspect of life. Her conduct springs, not from reasoning about moral questions, but from her concept of herself as a lady. In telling Henrietta that she is thinking of herself rather than Osmond she is stating the principle of her very being. Her concept owes something to the Protestant, perhaps even to the Puritan, tradition; and yet Isabel is a romantic, and the portrait of herself which she keeps before her is a romantic ideal. Her final choice—to return to Osmond and to Pansy, who needs her—is a free one. Yet the alternative is not really a life of comparative happiness with Goodwood, but the smashing of her ideal portrait of herself.

—Walter F. Wright, *The Madness of Art: A Study of Henry James* (Lincoln: University of Nebraska Press, 1962), pp. 147–48.

✣

J.I.M. Stewart on Isabel's Illusion of Freedom

[J.I.M. Stewart (1906–1994) was a lecturer at Christ Church College, Oxford, and a prolific literary critic. Among his critical works are *Rudyard Kipling* (1966) and *Thomas Hardy: A Critical Biography* (1971). Stewart also wrote many detective novels under the pen name Michael Innes. In *Eight Modern Writers* (1963), Stewart argues that Isabel's illusion of freedom is the subject of *The Portrait of a Lady.* He also comments on the role civility and breeding plays in the novel.]

The subject of *The Portrait of a Lady* is Isabel's illusion of freedom, where actually the whole course of her life is determined. Suddenly granted wealth and seeming independence, she thinks that she is laying hold on life. But really her cultural heritage—including the simple fact that she is a lady—is laying hold on her, and that heritage takes her back to Osmond in the end. James would appear to approve as well as chronicle his heroine's renunciation. He may even be charged with evoking a quasi-religious sanction for what is in fact an incidence of transcendentalized good form. For amid all the cheats and corruptions of European society by which, fondly and romantically admiring, his Americans are prone to be let down, there is one principle which their maturer experience will endorse as valid. It is the principle of keeping up appearances, of placing public decorum above private impulse. Beyond almost everything else, James and James's initiates prize that sort of breeding which enables a man or woman to preserve good formal manners despite every urgency of passion or emotion which may be assailing them. Nor is it hard to distinguish how James comes by this allegiance. When he condemned the large and impeccable art of Flaubert on the ground that it lacks moral dignity, he was naming his own ultimate value. But moral dignity appeared to him something fully viable only in the nourishing and sustaining medium of high civilization. And for James, as Sir Herbert Read has said, civilization meant "a perfectly definite historical phenomenon." It was what tradition and all the fine accumulations of time had given to the cultivated classes of western society in his own day. He was extremely sensitive to the material tokens by which this tradition asserted itself—although not perhaps so sensitive to them in detail and as individual works of art as aware of them in the gross as massively accumulated symbols of the idea. Hence his preoccupation with and deference towards grand or beautiful things and their owners. It seldom occurred to him that the attitude of the effective proprietors of these supremely significant objects could be one of vast inattention. He imagined—perhaps we must say in every sense—an aristocracy of culture so conscious of its tradition on the aesthetic side that its main business became that of living aesthetically up to it. These wonderful beings are intensely conscious that their wardenship of the tradition is a matter of sustained aesthetic perceptiveness in the fields alike of connoisseurship and conduct. The idea of style dominates the living of James's characters as much as it dominates that collecting of objets d'art with which they are, to our seeming, often so finically concerned. Hence the transcendentalizing of the idea of good form. It is not in itself moral dignity. But it is the touchstone of that perfected civility without which moral dignity is impossible. The idea does not permit Isabel to break even a quite common old plate over Osmond's head. It does not permit her to say, "Gilbert, I sometimes think—extravagant though it seems—that you are even more ridiculous than you are small and mean." And, not permitting this, it cannot permit her openly to turn away from him.

—J.I.M. Stewart, *Eight Modern Writers* (Oxford: The Clarendon Press, 1963), pp. 91–92.

✤

Elisabeth Luther Carey on the Role of Material Wealth in *The Portrait of a Lady*

[Elisabeth Luther Carey is an author and James scholar. In the following extract, taken from *The Novels of Henry James: A Study* (1964), Carey explores the significance of the rich material wealth that surrounds Isabel Archer in *The Portrait of a Lady*.]

In all the work of Mr. James we are conscious of a massive material splendour against which are thrown the shimmering reflections of character and temperament. However elusive these may be, the world we see about us is firm and rich as cloth of gold; and while money is infrequently given a prominent place in the discussion of human experience, the results of large, of immense expenditures are everywhere. The wealth of centuries is distilled in these wonderful houses, these private galleries of priceless art, these scattered, precious objects; while the magnificence of the social scale, the innumerable festivities, the vast, if not entirely noble hospitality, speak of great present incomes and a lavish disposition of them. The mere impression of assimilated and inexhaustible material resources is not, however, so uncommon in English fiction as to be especially worthy of note, unless with it we are shown a mode of thought or an attitude of mind to which the possession and consciousness of wealth bears an intimate relation.

It is not important in a world of acts and motives that people have money: it is greatly important what they do with it, and how they think of it, how it influences their lives and the lives of others. What is the temper of Mr. James's characters toward the solid substance of their fortunes, often of such heroic proportions? Do they hoard it, do they spend it with lack of thrift, do they give it away? It is suggestive to reflect that in the case of the Americans they chiefly give it away. In *The Portrait of a Lady*, that story of multitudinous threads, the attitude of Isabel Archer toward her inherited means indicates how literally, for her, money is means, the means in this instance of endowing a scoundrel,—but that is a matter apart. After receiving her uncle's legacy the question at once became how to get rid of it. But for her money she would not have married as she did:

> At bottom her money had been a burden, had been on her mind, which was filled with the desire to transfer the weight of it to some other conscience. What would lighten her own conscience more effectually than to make it over to the man who had the best taste in the world? Unless she should give it to a hospital, there was nothing better she could do with it; and there was no charitable institution in which she was as much interested as in Gilbert Osmond. He would use her fortune in a way that would make her think better of it, and rub off a certain grossness which attached to the good luck of an unexpected inheritance. There had been nothing very delicate in inheriting seventy thousand pounds; the delicacy had been all in Mr. Touchett's leaving them to her. But to marry Gilbert Osmond and bring him such a portion—in that there would be delicacy for her as well.
>
> —Elisabeth Luther Carey, *The Novels of Henry James: A Study* (New York: Haskell House, 1964), pp.119–22.

✤

Laurence Bedwell Holland on the Role of the Artist in *The Portrait of a Lady*

[Laurence Bedwell Holland (1920–1980) lectured at Princeton University and Johns Hopkins University. He is the author of *The Literary History of New Jersey* (1965) and the editor of *Who Designs America?* (1966).]

In the following article, taken from *The Expense of Vision: Essays on the Craft of Henry James*, Holland demonstrates how James's own explanations of *The Portrait of a Lady* led Holland to the conclusion that "self-recognition for the artist is central to the novel itself."]

The preface [to *The Portrait*] ⟨. . .⟩ is important not primarily as an explicit argument nor even as a statement of intentions but as a sensitive exploration, employing the instrument of metaphor, which moves beneath the more explicit discourse of the preface, refining and at times running counter to it. Its full relevance to the *Portrait*, and its brilliance as an essay in its own right, come to light only when read with full attention to its metaphorical details and to the intimate drama which moves implicitly within the more explicit argument. It becomes a conscience-stricken inquiry into the deepest implications of James's craft, undertaken at a time when, in preparing the revisions for the New York Edition of his fiction, James had engaged his mature creative powers in a direct confrontation of his imaginative work. What the preface can help us to see, if we follow the admittedly "long way round" it takes to get to its turning point, is that this process, a form of self-recognition for the artist, is central to the novel itself.

Indeed, the process of self-recognition is more penetrating in the *Portrait* than in the critical essays, or even those stories which deal with professional artists as particular cases, where we might be more tempted to look for it. And the *Portrait* speaks with the firm authority of a masterpiece and accordingly affords a commanding perspective on those occasions in James's career when he penetrated most deeply into his resources, his material and talent. It enables us to reexamine the connections among James's moral, social, and aesthetic themes in the light of his concern for form and to redefine James's relation to the society which has had to be interested, whether eagerly or reluctantly, in making and remaking things, in measuring the cost of human institutions and aspirations.

Of the many images of the artist which James employed, one of his favorites and most famous is that of the architect, but James's treatment of it in the preface to the *Portrait* accords it a curiously dubious status: the image does reveal some of James's deepest apprehensions about the act of imaginative vision but remains silent on the issue of "action" or the "nefarious" plot which most troubled him. The writer as architect, in his more public and active role, builds his structure, piling "brick upon brick" until, "scrupulously fitted together and packed in," they form the "large building" of the *Portrait*. The famous passage about the "house of fiction" develops the architectural image more amply, assigning to the artist a more private position inside a completed building and the ostensibly more restful occupation of a "watcher" whose sole activity is to observe: the "consciousness of the artist" stands behind the "dead wall" of a building enclosing him, equipped "with a pair of eyes, or at least with a field-glass," and scrutinizes life through the window of his particular literary form.

These architectural metaphors are relevant to the *Portrait*—if for no other reason than that they place the author inside his finished dwelling and call into question his edifice by alluding to its "dead wall"—yet the image of architecture does not dominate the preface because it does not satisfactorily come to grips with the assertion which James made the basis for the explicit argument of the preface. This is the assertion that the "figure" of Isabel (whatever its origin in James's acquaintanceship or reading) came first and alone without involvement in setting or action, an "unattached character" who was "not engaged in the tangle, to which we look for much of the impress that constitutes an identity." She was a "single character" given alone, as Turgenief had claimed his own were given, without the "situations" and "complications" which launch novels into "movement" and which identify a hero's world or "fate." The problem for the writer was, later, to "imagine, to invent and select and piece together . . . " the figure's world and "destiny."

—Laurence Bedwell Holland, *The Expense of Vision: Essays on the Craft of Henry James* (Princeton, NJ: Princeton University Press, 1964), pp. 3–5.

✤

John Rodenbeck on the Recurrent Image of the Bolted Door in *The Portrait of a Lady*

[John Rodenbeck is a literary critic and author who has taught at the University of Virginia and at the American University in Cairo. In an article from *Modern Fiction Studies*, Rodenbeck examines the recurrent image of the bolted door in *The Portrait of a Lady*.]

That Henry James was a great and conscious artist no one would think of denying. The aim of this paper is to contribute towards a statement of the exact nature of his consciousness by examining an incidentally recurring image in one of James's major novels and by demonstrating the fact that this image, though incidental, is so deliberately and thoroughly architected into the structure of the book that such an examination alone may provide a satisfactory reading of the novel as a whole. *The Portrait of a Lady* is epitomized, I want to show, in the recurrent image of the bolted door.

The Isabel Archer of the first half of the novel is an "intellectual," a bookworm. The important fact, until she meets Madame Merle, about every major incident to her life is that the incident itself comes as an interruption to her reading. The letter from Goodwood which she reads just before Warburton's proposal of marriage is, for example, a substitute for her usual diversions: "It seemed to her at last that she would do well to take a book; formerly, when heavy hearted, she had been able, with the help of some well-chosen volume, to transfer, the seat of consciousness to the organ of reason." When Goodwood himself arrives to make another proposal, she has been "trying to lose herself in a volume she had brought from Gardencourt." In the second half of the novel, on the other hand, Isabel attempts as far as we know to read no books until after Ralph's death: "She had never been less interested in literature than today; as she found when she occasionally took down from the shelf one of the rare and valuable volumes." By this time she cannot read. "There's nothing makes us so much alive as to see others die," Ralph has told her, and one of the great oppositions in the novel, certainly, is the opposition of the ideal rationality represented by books and the living consciousness of real life. *The Portrait of a Lady* records Isabel's steady weaning, then, from reading books to being wholly alive, from the solitude of intellectualism to the free individuality of an aristocratic self-realization. Ending for her as she stands on the verge of achievement, the novel begins with Isabel's solitary reading: "This young lady had been seated alone with a book. To say she was so occupied is to say her solitude did not press on her; for her love of knowledge had a fertilizing quality and her imagination was strong."

Mirrored in Isabel's mental engrossment with her book, which will never be equalled again, is the physical view she has from the little room in the house at Albany where Mrs. Touchett finds her so intellectually occupied.

> The place owed much of its mysterious melancholy to the fact that it was properly entered from the second door of the house, the door that had been condemned, and that was secured by bolts which a particularly slender little girl found it impossible to slide. She knew that this silent, motionless portal opened into the street; if the sidelights had not been filled with green paper she might have looked out on the little brown stoop and the well-worn brick pavement. But she had no wish to look out, for this would have interfered with her theory that there was a strange, unseen place on the other side—a place which became, to the child's imagination, according to its different moods, a region of delight or of terror.

Incapable of moving back the bolt that separates her from life, the early Isabel Archer prefers to live in her imagination, which is "by habit ridiculously active; when the door was not open it jumped out of the window. She was not indeed accustomed to keep it behind bolts; and at important moments, when she would have been thankful to make use of her judgment alone, she paid the penalty of having given undue encouragement to the faculty of seeing without judgment." It is her imagination, of course, her intellectuality, her extreme capacity for idealization, her "faculty of seeing without judgment" which in the second half of the novel brings Isabel a great deal of suffering and, in the end, a revivifying sense of life.

—John Rodenbeck, "The Bolted Door in James's *Portrait of a Lady*," *Modern Fiction Studies* 10, No. 4 (Winter 1964–65): 330–31.

Sister Lucy Schneider on Isabel Archer's Awakening Faith

[Sister Lucy Schneider, C.S.J., received her doctorate from the University of Notre Dame and contributed the article "Osculation and Integration: Isabel Archer in the One-Kiss Novel" to the *CLA Journal*. Here, Sister Schneider explores the significance of Caspar's love for Isabel and her return to Rome.]

Since its appearance in 1881, *The Portrait of a Lady* that Henry James penned has been studied from divers angles under a variety of lights. But whatever the angle, and whatever lighting in the literary gallery, the final view of *The Portrait* reveals Isabel Archer in the strong, hard arms of Caspar Goodwood, his lips on hers. Released from that embrace, she knows where to turn. "There was a very straight path . . . she started for Rome."

Why does Isabel return to Rome? To escape real love? Because she is not free to do otherwise? Neither of these answers seems satisfactory in the light—or lightning, rather—of Goodwood's kiss. I propose to answer the question by letting that kiss speak. It will say the final word, but not the only word. Granted, in a very real sense *The Portrait of a Lady* is, as the critics have said, a one-kiss novel; but actually many other kisses are recorded. As I see it, Isabel's return to Rome is to her previous experiences in her European adventure what Caspar's kiss is to the kisses that have preceded it. ⟨. . .⟩

Caspar loves her. Isabel is aware of that fact—deeply aware. He is sounding a heretofore unplumbed depth of her nature. But it is not her total nature. In Rome he had asked that he might pity her. She now begs him, with eyes streaming with tears, "As you love me, as you pity me, leave me alone!"

> He glared at her a moment through the dusk, and the next instant she felt his arms about her and his lips on her own lips. His kiss was like white lightning, a flash that spread, and spread again, and stayed; and it was extraordinarily as if, while she took it, she felt each thing in his hard manhood that had least pleased her, each aggressive fact of his face, his

figure, his presence, justified of its intense identity and made one with this act of possession.

When the "white lightning" was spent, Isabel moved, significantly "in an extraordinarily short time—for the distance was considerable—. . . through the darkness (for she saw nothing) and reached the door." Down the "very straight path" she will be marching to a processional that is not simply the "stately music that floated down from unknown periods in her husband's past," nor merely to the illusory melodies she thought she had heard, but rather to the full orchestra that each successive experience and realization have formed for her.

Osmond had once told her that if one is unhappy, he has himself to blame. Ralph had advised that she pay no attention to what people call her. "When you do suffer they call you an idiot." Within the framework of not very solidly based social and moral values—but very real values, nevertheless—"our heroine" has dropped the illusion that love means necessarily the absence of conflict. *In her own way* she has realized that Eros must tread the way of the Cross.

Was it only the "lightning" that struck the bench at Gardencourt that accounts for the "polygon's" smoothing into a circle? No, twenty lesser charges had previously formed a chain reaction in Isabel's feminine atmosphere to prepare for the final illuminating outburst. Isabel had said, "If a thing strikes me with a certain intensity, I accept it." What she is accepting is the "big view" and the "little fresh breeze" that Osmond claimed were the reward for climbing Goodwood's "tower." From this height Isabel does indeed see "the candlestick and the snuffers;" she sees Pansy; and she sees a scene that will last a lifetime. But this woman, this "idiot," follows the "very straight path," nevertheless. The seeming immurement and the suffering to which she returns constitute in reality the freedom to be the complete, loving woman—the strong woman of integrity she has, by degrees, become.

—Sister Lucy Schneider, C.S.J., "Osculation and Integration: Isabel Archer in the One-Kiss Novel," *CLA Journal* 10, No. 2 (December 1966): 149, 160–61.

NINA BAYM ON JAMES'S CHANGES TO THE FIRST DRAFTS OF *THE PORTRAIT OF A LADY*

[Nina Baym is the Liberal Arts and Sciences Jubilee Professor of English at the University of Illinois and an important literary critic. She is the author of *The Shape of Hawthorne's Career* (1976) and *Women's Fiction: A Guide to Novels by and About Women in America, 1820–1870* (1978). In the following excerpt, Baym explores the significance of James's revisions and thematic changes to *The Portrait of a Lady*.]

When Henry James revised *The Portrait of a Lady* for the New York Edition he made thousands of changes in the wording of the text. The revised version is stylistically and thematically closer to his later interests than the earlier one had been. Its writing is more complex, mannered, and metaphorical. It is thematically less timely and realistic, for its main concern is the private consciousness. In the 1908 version, Isabel Archer's inner life is the center of the character and of the novel's reality. In the early version the inner life is only one aspect of character, which is defined by behavior in a social context.

Owing to the prestige of the New York Edition, the novel of 1881 has largely been ignored by readers and critics, with a resulting loss in our sense of the early James as opposed to the later. In particular we do not see how topical and timely *The Portrait of a Lady* was. The 1881 novel was one of an increasing number of works about "the woman question." The heroine, an appealing young American, wants to live an independent and meaningful life; but she is thwarted. Unlike many works of the period on this theme, *The Portrait* did not depict Isabel's desire as unnatural and misguidedly unfeminine, nor did it employ the standard formula of saving her from this delusion by love and marriage. On the contrary, the novel sympathized with her aim to the point of calling both love and marriage into question. Moreover, it judged Isabel as limited by those inner qualities that, together with external obstacles, prevented her from pursuing and realizing her wish.

The changes of 1908, transforming the story into a drama of consciousness, overlaid and in places obliterated the coherence of the 1881 version. Omissions and additions altered all the characters significantly. Finally, James wrote a preface for the new work which announced that the story centered in the heroine's consciousness and that its action was the development of her perception and awareness. The preface instructed the reader how to interpret, what to admire, and what to deplore in the work. This preface is significant because it has largely controlled the critical readings of *The Portrait*. Since its interpretation works for 1908 but not so well for 1881, readers turning to the early version with the preface in mind naturally find an imperfect approximation of the revision. In case after case, passages which figure importantly in criticism of *The Portrait* occur in 1908 only. Strong arguments for Isabel's spiritual transcendence, and equally strong arguments for her hypocritical egotism, derive from that text. But the version of 1881 is a different work. Early James was a masterful writer with his own interests. Once recovered, the 1881 story with its topical focus on the "new woman" and its skillful use of fictional formulae, may prove to be just as interesting as the version of 1908.

The most extensive revisions concern Isabel Archer. She appears on almost every page of the book, and virtually every page about her undergoes change. Although some of these are only excisions or substitutions of single words, the cumulative effect is considerable. The chief intent of these changes is to endow her with the acute, subtle consciousness required for a late James work, which the early Isabel lacks. At the same time that James gives her a rich mental life in 1908, he effaces the original main quality of her character, emotional responsiveness. Her intellectual agility is greatly extended at the expense of her emotional nature.

From this basic change, others follow. Early Isabel is trapped by her simplicity; late Isabel must be the dupe of her subtlety. Victimized by an appeal to her highest faculties, she is less a fool than a saint. There is a corresponding change of tone to treat this more remarkable being. For example, "brilliant and noble" in 1881 becomes "high and splendid . . . and yet oh so radiantly gentle!" in 1908, while "a bright spirit" is rewritten as "a 'lustre' beyond any recorded losing or rediscovering." As

Isabel is exalted, other characters are degraded. Madame Merle and Osmond are thoroughly blackened, and many supporting figures are flattened and undercut by exaggerated comic treatment. The change in the two villains enhances the pathos of the situation of the trapped sensibility—Isabel Archer as redrawn is much more like Milly Theale than like the original Isabel Archer—while the minor characters lose their function as independent centers of judgment and awareness in the novel. When he is through, James has left nothing solid for the reader except the boundless imagination of Isabel. But in 1881 a limited imagination is her greatest shortcoming.

—Nina Baym, "Revision and Thematic Change in *The Portrait of a Lady*," *Modern Fiction Studies* 22, No. 2 (Summer 1976): 183–85.

ELIZABETH ALLEN ON THE WORLD OF APPEARANCES IN *THE PORTRAIT OF A LADY*

[Elizabeth Allen is a private sector official of the National Association of Teachers in Further and Higher Education in London. She is also the author of *A Woman's Place in the Novels of Henry James* (1984), from which the following was taken. Here, Allen explores the world of appearances in James's novel.]

In the opening chapters of *The Portrait of a Lady*, the constituent elements of the novel are established. Tea on the lawn at Gardencourt is made a vivid picture, yet at the same time we are made to feel how nothing here is "simply" pictorial. The timeless late afternoon links the old house with old Mr. Touchett, who loves the house and is aware of its past. A sense of social continuity is introduced into which Mr. Touchett, while retaining some detachment, knows where to slot. The sense of continuity is made present by a light-hearted discussion between the old man, Ralph and Lord Warburton, of impending social and political change. Mr. Touchett adds that social and political change, the fabric of day to day life, won't affect the "ladies," at least not those who really are ladies: "The ladies will save us," said the old man; "that is the best of them will—for I make a difference between them."

The best of the ladies, the most purely "lady"like of them, are not affected by the day to day adjustments of active participation in life—better than this, and immutable, they exist for the active participants in society as fixed reference points outside the expediency of a world which requires ideals at a safe distance. The extent to which this particular status for the ladies may be idealized or merely representative of worldly qualities is suggested in the discussion of the American girl that Mrs. Touchett has mentioned in her telegram. She has hinted at her being independent—the response of the tea party is to wonder whether it is financial or moral independence that is to be surveyed in this new arrival.

When Isabel arrives, her difference is quickly marked out by her prime activity—while they, and we, are surveying her, she is surveying everything. She has "an eye that denoted clear perception," her face is "intelligent and excited" with "a comprehensiveness of observation," her "perceptions were numerous." Isabel is looking at everything, and as we look at her through Ralph's eyes we see:

> her white hands, in her lap, were folded upon her black dress; her head was erect, her eye lighted, her flexible figure turned itself easily this way and that, in sympathy with the alertness with which she evidently caught impressions.

The extent to which perception at this stage in the novel equates with static pictures and impressions is evident both in others' sense of Isabel and in Isabel's sense of them and herself. Awareness of appearances is primary, and exists long before the understanding of such appearances. In *Ways of Seeing*, John Berger analyses the way in which men, as spectators of women in pictures, turn women into spectators of themselves, in order to monitor their existence for the external world, to try and gain some "self" control from the inside of the system that controls them: "Men survey women before treating them. Consequently how a woman appears to a man can determine how she will be treated."

Isabel instinctively interiorizes the process of being seen as an attempt at control, and tries to present herself (and to see others) in a very fine abstract way. She is concerned with her appearance as feminine—we are told that she doesn't want to be thought "bookish" but "clever," and that she is aware of the importance of prettiness. But this awareness of her feminine self is carried over into a sense of transcendent femininity, a moral harmony of appearance. Isabel determines then that "Her life should always be in harmony with the most pleasing impression she should produce." It is in expectation of a judgment on her moral character as well as her appearance that she desires to "look very well."

By projecting an active, spiritual appearance to the world, Isabel apparently hopes to keep her options open. Though she herself sees others as types, they are often types expressive of wide ideas—Lord Warburton as the English social system, Henrietta as American democracy—and if she projects herself as a general enough range of significations her chances of appropriation might be less. For she is afraid of the "ruinous expenditure" of giving herself to another person.

Unfortunately in a world of appearances not necessarily highlighted by a qualitative perception, others may see one in a more limiting way. This is not necessarily a product of malice; we are told of Mr. Touchett, who is very fond of Isabel, that she: "amused him more than she suspected—the effect she produced on people was often different from what she supposed."

This concept of entertainment, of watching Isabel to see what will happen, of seeing her as a series of images from which amusement can be derived, is present in all the Touchetts. Their fondness for Isabel, and willingness to help, their restraint from actual manipulation, disguises the shortcomings of this approach. And in comparison to the more specific appropriation practiced by other characters, this spectatorship is not so harmful. Nonetheless it turns Isabel into a performer, and heightens the sense of her as an image of free womanhood, as a principle in action. Ralph is exonerated in a sense by having the role of spectator forced on him by ill health. He, like Warburton and Goodwood, would be willing to involve himself with Isabel rather than just watch her, if he only could. However, confined to watching, he does so very thoroughly. He views Isabel as "occupation enough for a succession of days," and considers that "she was better worth looking at than most works of art."

—Elizabeth Allen, *A Woman's Place in the Novels of Henry James* (New York: St. Martin's Press, 1984), pp. 62–64.

✤

TONY TANNER ON MADAME MERLE AND OSMOND

[Tony Tanner is the director of English Studies at King's College, Cambridge, and an important literary scholar. Among his publications are *Conrad's Lord Jim* (1963), *Saul Bellow* (1965), and *City of Words: American Fiction, 1950–1970* (1971). The following selection from *Henry James: The Writer and His Work* (1985) includes Tanner's exploration of the roles of Madame Merle and Osmond.]

Madame Merle—the blackbird—is Osmond's partner in plotting, and she has acquired such an apparently civilized veneer that Isabel is still American enough to feel she is "not natural." Yet in many ways she wishes to emulate Madame Merle's total self-control and cool detachment (Madame Merle's most chilling remark is "I don't pretend to know what people are for. . . . I only know what I can do with them"). These two ladies have one exchange that is crucial to the book. It starts when Isabel says that she does not care what kind of house Caspar Goodwood has. Madame Merle's answer is central. "'That's very crude of you. When you've lived as long as I have you'll see that every human has his shell and you must take that shell into account. By the shell I mean the whole envelope of circumstances. There's no such thing as an isolated man or woman; we're each of us made up of some cluster of appurtenances. What shall we call our "self"? Where does it begin? Where does it end? It overflows into everything that belongs to us—and then it flows back again. I know a large part of myself is the clothes I choose to wear. I've a great respect for *things*! One's self—for other people—is one's expression of one's self; and one's house, one's furniture, one's garments, the books one reads, the company one keeps—these things are all expressive.'" Now, there is a great deal in this that is true, but Isabel immediately disagrees. "'I don't agree with you. I think just the other way. I don't know whether I succeed in expressing myself, but I know that nothing can express me; everything's on the contrary a limit, a barrier, and a perfectly arbitrary one. Certainly the clothes which, as you say, I choose to wear, don't express me; and heaven forbid they should. . . . My clothes may express the dressmaker, but they don't express me. To begin with it's not my own choice that I wear them; they're imposed on me by society.'

'Should you prefer to go without them?' Madame Merle enquired in a tone which virtually terminated the discussion."

Isabel is very American in her suspicion of "things" as "limits" and her idea of a pure self existing apart from all materiality. But without limits you cannot have identity. And while the self is not *identical* with things, Madame Merle is right to the extent that the self must enter into commerce with things (houses, clothes, other people, etc.) to establish itself as a self and experience itself as a self. There is no self in a void. The danger, of course, is when things absorb the self, and the self abandons itself to thinghood. Isabel is dangerously one-sided—and vulnerable—in what she thinks of as her contempt for the encircling things that make up her world as much as they do anybody else's.

It is partly this error that brings her into Osmond's "prison" while she thought she had been discovering her liberty. 〈. . .〉 Isabel—with her own system, her theory of freedom, has been engorged and trapped by Osmond's more rigid system which seeks to make over other people for his own use, transforming them into things for his manipulation (as he does with his daughter Pansy). Isabel's crime is "having a mind of her own." He cannot tolerate the otherness of free-standing people.

It is part of the characteristic atmosphere of the book that, while Isabel develops in her own way and sight deepens into insight, there is a growing feeling of free spontaneous life giving way, or turning into, mechanistic automata, art objects, instruments, masks, theatrical performances, shells containing no life. People become dry and empty, touched or blighted with that desiccation that for Shakespeare was a mark of evil or dead life—as when Madame Merle complains to Osmond, "you've dried up my soul." Even Isabel, near the end, goes into something like a catatonic state, devoid of "purpose [and] intention," envying statues and objects their insentient immobility, longing, even, for death. In particular, this mood afflicts her as she is on her way to see Ralph who is dying—she has gone against Osmond's express desire that she shouldn't, but to her he scarcely exists as a human being any more. And to Ralph, arguably the one true lover in the book, she finally comes, and a moving deathbed scene ensues. "She had lost all her shame, all wish to hide things. Now he must know; she wished him to know, for it brought them supremely together." When she says she would die not to lose him he answers: "You won't lose me—you'll keep me. Keep me in your heart. I shall be nearer to you than I've ever been. Dear Isabel, life is better; for in life there's love. Death is good—but there's no love." And he ends by assuring her "if you've been hated you've also been loved. Ah but, Isabel—*adored*!" And in a moment of recognition of her truest allegiance she answers, "Oh my brother!"

—Tony Tanner, *Henry James: The Writer and His Work* (Amherst: University of Massachusetts Press, 1985), pp. 44–46.

✤

Deborah Esch on James as a Critic of His Own Work

[Deborah Esch is an assistant Professor of English at Princeton and an author. Here, Esch explores the significance of James's "Preface" to *The Portrait of a Lady* and James's role as a critic of his own work.]

Ever a vigilant critic of his own work as well as that of other writers, James frequently took occasion in his essays and prefaces to remark on the exigencies of what was for him "the most difficult, the most delicate," "the most complicated and the most particular" of the arts. In "The Science of Criticism," written for the *New Review* in May 1891, and reprinted in 1893 under the abbreviated title "Criticism," he reflected on the intellectual and affective "outfit" required for work in the critical spirit, and granted that

> one is ready to pay almost any homage to the intelligence that has put it on; and when one considers the noble figure completely equipped—armed *cap à pie* in curiosity and sympathy—one falls in love with the apparition. It certainly represents the knight who has knelt through his long vigil and who has the piety of his office.

The essay further pursues the metaphor of the vigil, and in its closing line supplies a further analogy for the activity of criticism:

> Any vocation has its hours of intensity that is so closely connected with life. That of the critic, in literature, is connected doubly, for he deals with life at second-hand as well as at first; that is, he deals with the experience of others, which he resolves into his own, and not of those invented and selected others with whom the novelist makes comfortable terms, but with the uncompromising swarm of authors, the clamorous children of history. . . . We must be easy with him if the picture, even when the aim has really been to penetrate, is sometimes confused, for there are baffling and there are thankless subjects; and we make everything up to him by the particular purity of our esteem when the portrait is really, like the happy portraits of the other art, a text preserved by translation.

The analogy with the "other art," like the earlier metaphor of the vigil, directs the reader of these reflections to *The Portrait of a Lady*. Isabel Archer, the lady imagined in the titular portrait, proves to be "connected doubly" with criticism, in a doubleness signalled in the pivotal genitive of the novel's title: she is arguably its object—its text—as well as its subject—its reader. In the first extended account of his heroine in the novel's sixth chapter, *The Portrait*'s narrator caps a catalogue of her virtues and flaws with the observation that "she would be an easy victim of scientific criticism if she were not intended to awaken on the reader's part an impulse more tender and more purely expectant." In these terms, echoed elsewhere in the novel, Isabel figures the text, and her "portrait" becomes, according to the analogy of the essay on criticism, more precisely a text preserved by translation. On the other hand, in the chapter singled out by James in the preface to *The Portrait* as "obviously the best thing in the book," and "a supreme illustration of the general plan," Isabel herself takes up the "extraordinary meditative vigil," the "vigil of searching criticism." What Richard Poirier, in an account of the heroine as a figure for the author, represents as Isabel's "whole effort at self-creation, the impulse which makes her into a kind of novelist of her own experience," in James's terms culminates in the lady's assuming the stance of the critical "knight" of his own analogy—the position of a vigilant reader attempting to interpret a text—in this case, the text of her own past. Isabel's "hours of intensity" by the dying fire in chapter 42 attest to her critical vocation, baffling and thankless as it proves. To trace the consequences of her "double connection" to criticism, to mark its rhythm of alternation in the novel, is, for James's reader, to begin to account for the complexity of the "portraiture" in question.

—Deborah Esch, "'Understanding Allegories': Reading *The Portrait of a Lady*," *Henry James's The Portrait of a Lady*, ed. Harold Bloom (New York: Chelsea House Publishers, 1987), pp. 131–32.

WILLIAM VEEDER ON THE ASSOCIATION OF TRANSIENCE WITH MORTALITY IN *THE PORTRAIT OF A LADY*

[William Veeder is a literary critic and author; among his publications are *W. B. Yeats: The Rhetoric of Repetition* (1968) and *Henry James: The Lessons of the Master, Popular Fiction and Personal Style in the Nineteenth Century* (1975). In the following extract, Veeder explores the connection between transience and mortality in *The Portrait of a Lady*.]

The association of transience with mortality which we have seen in *A Small Boy* recurs in the opening of *The Portrait*, as flux leads to death. The mortal illnesses of Daniel and Ralph Touchett sign them as negated from the start. Daniel "was not likely to displace himself," Ralph "was not very firm on his legs" (Chap. 1). The fact that disease is established before love enters the novel is important: fatal women do not cause male inadequacy in *The Portrait*. Warburton may suggest such causation when he tells Isabel, "if you refuse me . . . I shall live to no purpose" (Chap. 12), but Warburton has had no purpose from the first. Though he seems healthy next to Daniel and Ralph, Warburton too is sick. "'He is sick of life'" (Chap. 1). Warburton's negation is political, for "'he doesn't take himself seriously . . . and he doesn't know what to believe in . . . [he] can neither abolish himself as a nuisance nor maintain himself as an institution'" (Chap. 8). Warburton admits "'I don't approve of myself the least'" (Chap. 14). The fact that political negation constitutes, in effect, the condition of "woman" is confirmed when Warburton goes on to equate himself, however ironically, with his powerless sister. "'We neither of us have any position to speak of'" (Chap. 14). Association with another powerless woman is prepared for in the first scene, where Warburton wears "a hat which looked too big for him" (Chap. 1). Pansy too wears a "hat [which] always seemed too big for her" (Chap. 35). That "'she does not really fill out the part'" (Chap. 37) is equally true of Warburton, as Isabel confirms. "'I said she [Pansy] was limited. And so she is. And so is Lord Warburton'" (Chap. 40).

That emasculate men inhabit the condition of the feminine is confirmed in the opening description of the tea drinkers. "They were not of the sex which is supposed to furnish the regular votaries of the ceremony" (Chap. 1). In the face of woman's traditional definition as the nonmale, men here in *The Portrait* are defined as the nonfemale—*at the very moment that the females are marked as absent.* Lydia, who should preside over the tea ceremony, is not here; Isabel, who could substitute for her, has not yet arrived on the lawn. To be the negative of the absent does not give presence to men, for the lengthening shadows emblematic of mortality "were the shadows of an old man sitting . . . and of two younger men strolling" (Chap. 1). Transience and consequent negation are epitomized by one of the shadows, Ralph Touchett, who "'does nothing.' . . . there was really nothing he had wanted very much to do, so that he had given up nothing" (Chap. 5). That men reduced to Ralph's "'mere spectatorship'" (Chap. 15) are worse off, are less than, women is emphasized by Madame Merle. "'A woman, perhaps, can get on. . . . But the men . . . what do they make of it over here? I don't envy them, trying to arrange themselves. Look at poor Ralph Touchett . . . "an American who lives in Europe." That signifies absolutely nothing'" (Chap. 19). ⟨. . .⟩ Most important, and possibly most surprising, Ralph is like Gilbert Osmond. "'He does nothing' . . . 'I could do nothing' . . . 'What is he? Nothing at all but a very good man. He is not in business'" (Chap. 10, 24, 32). Our difficulty in distinguishing Ralph from Gilbert (who is the subject of all the clauses except the first) has its counterpart when Daniel Touchett says of his son what proves to be true of Osmond: "'You look at things in a way that could make everything wrong'" (Chap. 18). We readers agree of course with Isabel's distinction "that Ralph was generous and her husband was not" (Chap. 42), but this distinction must be earned in the face of important similarities between the two men.

These similarities, moreover, implicate expatriate women as well. Both genders in *The Portrait* negate life by turning persons into objects. This reifying penchant, which is unmistakable in Osmond—he defines Isabel as "'a young lady who had qualified herself to figure in his collection of choice objects'" (Chap. 28)—also characterizes Ralph, who initially sees Isabel as "'a Titian, by the post, to hang on my wall'" (Chap. 7). ⟨. . .⟩ That Isabel is an object for women as well as for men is evident when Ralph celebrates spectatorship.

> "I shall have the entertainment of seeing what a young lady does who won't marry Lord Warburton."
>
> "That is what your mother counts upon too," said Isabel.
>
> "Ah, there will be plenty of spectators! We shall contemplate the rest of your career."

The "gaze" is not exclusively masculine in *The Portrait*, as it is in so much of Western culture. When Merle says to Isabel, "'I want to see what life makes of you'" (Chap. 19), she forsees direct entertainment for Osmond and indirect profit for herself. Both sexes are unable not to treat human beings as objects because both sexes sense their own essential reification. Without a positive sense of one's own subjectivity, one cannot value the other as subject, as sacredly other. Being essentially negated is what expatriation represents for both sexes. "'If we are not good Americans we are certainly poor Europeans; we have no natural place here'" (Chap. 19).

—William Veeder, "The Portrait of a Lack," *New Essays on The Portrait of a Lady*, ed. Joel Porte (New York: Cambridge University Press, 1990), pp. 106–8.

✤

LYALL H. POWERS ON ISABEL AS A "TYPICAL AMERICAN"

[Lyall H. Powers is a professor of English at the University of Michigan and a literary critic. Among his publications are *Henry James: An Introduction and Interpretation* (1970) and *Henry James and the Naturalist Movement* (1971). In this extract from *The Portrait of a Lady: Maiden, Woman, and Heroine* (1991), Powers explores Isabel's innocence and James's description of her as a "typical American."]

A critical reading of *The Portrait of a Lady* might begin with the lead provided by James's preface. He says there that "the germ of my idea" consisted "not at all in any conceit of a 'plot,' nefarious name," but "altogether in the sense of a single character, the character and aspect of a particular engaging young woman, to which all the usual elements of a 'subject,' certainly a setting, were to need to be super-added." The emphasis is on the importance of character, of the engaging young Isabel Archer, but we note the distinction made between character and plot—that is, between picture and action or *stasis* and movement—although James recognizes the need for both.

The novel opens with the careful preparation for the effective dramatic entrance of the main character: the scene is an almost ideal setting for the ceremony of afternoon tea, and all the gentlemen present are anticipating the arrival of the interesting girl from America. They know she is "quite independent," but they aren't sure what that means. She makes her dramatic entrance, framed for a moment in the doorway leading to the garden, all eyes focused upon her; she remains the focus of the story. The dramatic—or theatrical—mode continues as James allows Isabel to characterize herself by her words and actions; he himself gives very little interpretive comment.

The three gentlemen are immediately taken by her, and even the dogs are at once captivated, as though they sympathize with her natural goodness. She quickly proves herself to be innocent and naive and charming as well as independent-minded. Her romantic outlook is revealed when cousin Ralph introduces her to Lord Warburton and she responds, "Oh, I hoped there would be a lord; it's just like a novel!" The note of independence is soon sounded as the question of the length of her visit is raised. She first replies, appropriately, "My aunt must settle that"; then—

> "I'll settle it with her—at a quarter to seven." And Ralph looked at his watch again.
>
> "I'm glad to be here at all," said the girl.
>
> "I don't believe you allow things to be settled for you."
>
> "Oh yes; if they're settled as I like them."

And as Ralph suggests that Mrs. Touchett has adopted her, Isabel remarks that she is "not a candidate for adoption": "I'm very fond of my liberty."

In the next three chapters of flashback the character of Isabel is given historical substantiation; we are introduced briefly to the young man in Isabel's life, Caspar Goodwood, in terms that we will recall frequently in the course of the novel: "he was a straight young man from Boston . . . tall, strong, and somewhat stiff." There is also a sketch of Ralph, an American who was educated in England as well, thus "English enough," but "His outward conformity to the manners that surrounded him was none the less the mask of a mind that greatly enjoyed its independence, on which nothing long imposed itself." Independent-minded Ralph is an apt cousin and friend for Isabel—and the novel will test that appropriate relationship. ⟨. . .⟩

It is tempting to call Isabel a typical American—James might seem to be doing so—and to categorize her as "Emersonian."

She is fond of her freedom and of making her own choices, apparently self-reliant. Yet there is another side to Isabel, inescapably: with all her independent-mindedness there is a certain reluctance to confront life. We remember her thanking Mrs. Touchett for telling her she should not sit alone with gentlemen in the evening and other things one shouldn't do. "So as to do them?" asks her aunt. "So as to choose," is Isabel's cool reply. Yet we know that from her earliest years the reluctance to face experience, a kind of cherishing of her ignorance, has marked Isabel. She liked the office beyond the library, in her family home in Albany; but there was a bolted door that gave onto the street: "But she had no wish to look out, for this would have interfered with her theory that there was a strange, unseen place on the other side—a place which became to the child's imagination, according to its different moods, a region of delight and terror." Although she claims to Ralph that she is fond of knowledge, he is correct in his response: "Yes, of happy knowledge—of pleasant knowledge. But you haven't suffered, and you're not meant to suffer. I hope you never see the ghost!"

—Lyall H. Powers, *The Portrait of a Lady: Maiden, Woman, and Heroine* (Boston: Twayne Publishers, 1991), pp. 33–34, 35.

✤

JONATHAN WARREN ON ISABEL'S PAST AND FUTURE

[Jonathan Warren, a literary critic and author, teaches at the University of Toronto. In the following extract, Warren explores the nature of time and Isabel's quest for freedom.]

Isabel's past and present have been a never-changing appeal to her futurity. How, then, can she imagine a disjunction between past, present, and future coming, as she does, from a history of profound temporal sameness? Moreover, Isabel acts in accordance with the structure that has defined her past: she promises. Isabel translates herself from imminent to actual through a future-oriented act and thus masks the disjunction inherent in her translation. She has agonizingly refused the proposal of Warburton and postponed the advances of Goodwood because both seemed preclusive, somehow contrary to her vast potential; her history has been one of postponement. Why should a promise of marriage to Gilbert Osmond, himself the putatively unpreclusive unknown quantity, which Isabel conceives as furtherance of her vast potential, be read by her as anything else? Isabel acts—exercises her personal promise (potential), by promising—and, thus, disguises any discrepancy between her potential and her vow, her promise and her promise, in continued delusions of immanent imminence and an eternal moment of multitudinous purposes. After her marriage to Osmond, and before chapter 42, Isabel is deluded that her fate continues suspended and imminent while she has actually entered a diachronic time and, through that entrance, has violently disjoined herself from her office—her immanence, her identity, and her past.

Isabel trusts Madame Merle and Gilbert Osmond not a little because of the manner of their temporal self-portrayal that duplicitously appeals to the eternal; it seems to Isabel that they are as they always have been. Why should we think, knowing her history, that Isabel would or could imagine otherwise? Madame Merle and Osmond dissemble, suggesting and saying that they are as they always have been. Isabel accepts Osmond as a man with "[n]o career, no name, no position, no fortune, no past, no future, no anything." She shrinks "from raising curtains and looking into unlighted corners" in an expression of her fine capacity for ignorance, which is linked to her sense of the stasis in which she imagines she exists. If everything is as it always has been, then there is no possibility even for the imagination of treachery: treachery depends on the plotting which requires diachrony. Isabel still imagines her potential as vast even though her future and Madame Merle's treachery have become contingent. The idyll of a carriage careering into the directionless dark continues to inform Isabel's fancy: "She [Isabel] had always been fond of history, and here was history in the stones of the street and the atoms of the sunshine. She had an imagination that kindled at the mention of great deeds, and wherever she turned some great deed had been acted. . . . Her consciousness was so mixed that she scarcely knew where the different parts of it would lead her, and she went about in a repressed ecstasy of contemplation." However, her ecstasy of contemplation in the dark gives way to apprehension about the mysteries of the unknown. 〈. . .〉

Isabel finally discerns a discrepancy in what she had assumed is still an historical eternal that does not allow for any disjunction of past and present realities during her oft-discussed vigil in chapter 42. Alone with the furniture in the darkness, as we have seen her before, Isabel concludes this chapter lingering over an image that rends the fabric of eternity: Madame Merle and Gilbert Osmond have, simply, not always been as they now seem. The stunning revelations of Countess Gemini do not come for nine more chapters. It would seem, then, that before she learns of the substance of the discrepancy in Merle's and Osmond's past, and of the treachery it precipitates, Isabel is chiefly struck by the structural incongruence of a treachery and the diachrony that it requires.

Isabel shares an affinity with Gilbert Osmond's daughter that is not sufficiently explained by characterization alone. That Pansy exists in a cloistered suspension among the good sisters and in a sort of perversely constant prepubescence by her father, who has her in skirts that are always too short and hats that are always too large, recalls Isabel's own stasis in a most gruesome way. Pansy is described early on as a *tabula rasa*; her "absence of initiative, of conversation, of personal claims, seem[s] . . . in a girl of twenty, unnatural and even uncanny." Pansy lives in an eternal moment just as Isabel seemed to before her marriage. Pansy, unlike Isabel, however, is not said to have a vast potential; instead, we see that her desire is singular: it is the love of Ned Rosier denied by her father. Isabel's difficult advocacy of this young romance occupies the interval between her realization of a redefinitive historical schism, involving Merle and Osmond, and her final promise to Pansy. This project, though less than successful, forces Isabel to confront with unease the ramifications of an imposed static posture. That is, Pansy's forced indefinite postponement of her life recalls Isabel's own office. It is unclear whether or not Isabel draws the analogy—we are told that she is "incapable of that large inward reference, the tone almost of the philosophic historian"—but I find it all-important that the heroine who supremely valorizes her freedom to forget is assigned at least one crucial remembrance in this regard: Isabel remembers Pansy.

—Jonathan Warren, "Imminence and Immanence: Isabel Archer's Temporal Predicament in *The Portrait of a Lady*." *The Henry James Review* 14; No. 1 (Winter 1993): 10–12.

Kelly Cannon on Ralph Touchett's Disability and Its Relation to Sexual Pleasure

[Kelly Cannon is a critic and James scholar. She is the author of *Henry James and Masculinity: The Man at the Margins* (1994), from which the following extract was taken. Here, Cannon argues that Ralph Touchett's disability leads him toward voyeurism in a quest for sexual pleasure.]

Perhaps no other male character stands so obviously bereft of normal sexual pleasures as does Ralph Touchett, whose physical disability makes him avoid marriage, though he doesn't appear to resent bachelorhood. Like the marginal males mentioned, Ralph Touchett finds pleasure elsewhere, in his case from what may best be termed voyeurism, as he enjoys watching the pleasure of others, in particular Isabel's romantic pursuits. He says to her, "I content myself with watching you—with deepest interest." James depicts a man who at a young age has a diminished physical capacity, and who accordingly commits himself to a life of passivity, forbidding himself the "arts of demonstration." The pleasure afforded Touchett may never brink that of sexual orgasm, but the pleasure he derives is nonetheless intense.

Indeed, orgasm is not considered "an essential part of . . . voyeurism"; the voyeur enjoys a more nebulous "erotic gratification" or "satisfaction." The voyeur, or "scopophiliac," finds pleasure in viewing the gratification of another person, and is additionally gratified by a sense of power over the object of that gaze because the voyeur takes enjoyment from an unwilling and often unwitting partner, feasting as he does with the eyes. The partner may feel drained by the intensity of the voyeur's gaze, though he or she may gain if the ego is complimented by the gaze; however, if the gaze exceeds the boundaries of the partner's pleasure, the partner becomes victim rather than beneficiary, feeling trapped and powerless to incriminate the voyeur. Indeed, the pleasure of the voyeur is among the safest forms of sexual gratification for the perpetrator. "The stance of detached contemplation" provides "compensatory" eroticism that "relieves" the contemplator of "the burden of suffering that can come with more direct involvement." It is difficult to convict someone for voyeurism or peeping because "there is no victim contact and the offender usually is not seen at all." The object of the gaze can never attaint the voyeur except on grounds of suspicion. In this way, the voyeur loses nothing.

These features of voyeurism surface in the way Ralph watches Isabel Archer. As the reader is told in *The Portrait of a Lady*, Ralph "lost nothing, in truth, by these wandering glances." Ralph's gaze is fixed on Isabel: "He noticed everything that Isabel did." On one occasion Isabel demands that Ralph leave her so that she can be alone for a "simple and solitary repast." He pleads with her to let him remain, and she replies, "No, you will dine at your club." The reader is then privileged to know Ralph's feelings at that moment: "It would have given him extreme pleasure to be present in person at the modest little feast she had sketched."

He settles, however, for those few moments when he can be with her prior to her meal. His feelings here are characteristic of the voyeur, who learns to settle for whatever vista is offered him. The fuel of the voyeur's desire resides in a desire for satisfactions passively acquired with little or no risk. Ralph acknowledges at this moment precisely what his compensatory satisfactions are, and revels in them.

> For the moment, however, he liked immensely being alone with her, in the thickening dusk, in the centre of the multitudinous town; it made her seem to depend upon him and be in his power. This power he could exert but vaguely; the best exercise of it was to accept her decisions submissively. There was almost an emotion in doing so.

In Ralph's weighing of the situation, in his careful extraction of pleasure from what remains, his occupation as voyeur represents the paradigm of sexual surprise—maximum pleasure at minimum risk.

Most readers can only wonder at what compensations the voyeur finds. Ralph's father cannot understand, having lived a normal life as a functional heterosexual male. Daniel's is the aggressive life, having obtained wealth after having filled the preconditions of marriage and children, and so he naturally wishes that his son would follow in his footsteps, and in particular that he would marry. Ralph refuses and requests instead that half his fortune be given to Isabel. Deeply disturbed, Daniel tries to convince his son of the absurdity of his request, saying in reproach, "You speak as if it were for your entertainment." Ralph admits, "I shall get just the good that I said just now I wished to put in Isabel's reach—that of having gratified my imagination." (James describes Ralph as a man who seeks "his entertainment wherever he could find it.")

Discovering Ralph's secret gratification, Isabel questions him. In defense, Ralph says, "Of course you mean that I am meddling in what doesn't concern me." Troubled by the sensitivity of the subject, he asks, "Why shouldn't I speak to you of this matter without annoying you or embarrassing myself?" The law of the voyeur forbids verbalization; speaking about voyeurism robs the activity of its unique advantage of secrecy. Isabel's having found him out means a possible loss of his vantage point. "Ralph . . . had wished to see for himself; but while he was engaged in this pursuit he felt afresh what a fool he had been to put the girl on her guard." In lamenting his lost advantage, Ralph reveals the intensity of his desire to see "all."

His passionate defense assures both Isabel and the reader that his voyeuristic activities are necessary to him. His pleasure is no game, but his very *raison d'etre*. He says to Isabel, "What is the use of adoring you without the hope of a reward, if I can't have a few compensations? What is the use of being ill and disabled, and restricted to mere spectatorship at the game of life, if I really can't see the show when I have paid so much for my ticket?" Ralph brandishes emotional appeal with great skill as he tries to justify behavior that to Isabel must seem ludicrous.

—Kelly Cannon, *Henry James and Masculinity: The Man at the Margins* (New York: St. Martin's Press, 1994), pp. 87–90.

✤

Works by Henry James

A Passionate Pilgrim. 1875.

Transatlantic Sketches. 1875.

Roderick Hudson. 1875.

The American. 1877.

French Poets and Novelists. 1878.

Watch and Ward. 1878.

The Europeans. 1878.

Daisy Miller. 1878.

An International Episode. 1879.

The Madonna of the Future. 1879.

Confidence. 1879.

Hawthorne. 1879.

The Diary of a Man of Fifty. 1880.

Washington Square. 1880.

The Portrait of a Lady. 1881.

Daisy Miller: A Comedy. 1883.

The Siege of London. 1883.

Portraits of Places. 1883.

A Little Tour in France. 1884.

Tales of Three Cities. 1884.

The Author of "Beltraffio." 1885.

Stories Revived. 1885.

The Bostonians. 1886.

The Princess Casamassima. 1886.

Partial Portraits. 1888.

The Reverberator. 1888.

The Aspern Papers. 1888.

A London Life. 1889.

The Tragic Muse. 1890.

The Lesson of the Master. 1892.

The Real Thing. 1893.

Picture and Text. 1893.

The Private Life. 1893.

Essays in London and Elsewhere. 1893.

The Wheel of Time. 1893.

Theatricals. 1894.

Terminations. 1895.

Theatricals: Second Series. 1895.

Embarrassments. 1896.

The Other House. 1896.

The Spoils of Poynton. 1897.

What Maisie Knew. 1897.

In the Cage. 1898.

The Two Magics. 1898.

The Awkward Age. 1899.

The Soft Side. 1900.

The Sacred Fount. 1901.

The Wings of the Dove. 1902.

The Better Sort. 1903.

The Ambassadors. 1903.

William Wetmore Story and His Friends. 1903.

The Golden Bowl. 1904.

English Hours. 1905.

The American Scene. 1907.

The Novels and Tales of Henry James. 1907–9.

Views and Reviews. 1908.

Julia Bride. 1909.

Italian Hours. 1909.

The Finer Grain. 1910.

The Outcry. 1911.

A Small Boy and Others. 1913.

Notes of a Son and Brother. 1914.

Notes on Novelists. 1914.

The Ivory Tower. 1917.

The Sense of the Past. 1917.

The Middle Years. 1917.

Gabrielle de Bergerac. 1918.

Within the Rim. 1919.

Master Eustace. 1920.

Travelling Companions. 1919.

A Landscape Painter. 1920.

Works About Henry James and *The Portrait of a Lady*

Agnew, Jean-Christophe. "The Consuming Vision of Henry James." In *The Culture of Consumption: Critical Essays in American History, 1880–1980*, ed. Richard Wightman Fox and T. J. Jackson Lears. New York: Pantheon, 1983, pp. 67–100.

Allott, Miriam. "Form Versus Substance in Henry James." *The Review of English Literature* 3, No. 1 (1962): 53–66.

Anderson, Charles. *Person, Place, and Thing in Henry James's Novels*. Durham, NC: Duke University Press, 1977.

Anderson, Quentin. *The American Henry James*. New Brunswick, NJ: Rutgers University Press, 1957.

Banta, Martha. *Henry James and the Occult: The Great Extension*. Bloomington: Indiana University Press, 1972.

Berland, Alwyn. *Culture and Conduct in the Novels of Henry James*. Cambridge: Cambridge University Press, 1981.

Bewley, Marius. *The Complex Fate*. London: Chatto & Windus, 1952.

Blackmur, R. P. *Studies in Henry James*. New York: New Directions, 1983.

Booth, Bradford A. "Henry James and the Economic Motif." *Nineteenth-Century Fiction* 8 (September 1953): 141–50.

Brooks, Van Wyck. *The Pilgrimage of Henry James*. New York: Dutton, 1925.

Cargill, Oscar. *The Novels of Henry James*. New York: Macmillan, 1961.

Chase, Richard. *The American Novel and Its Traditions*. Garden City, NY: Doubleday, 1957.

Crews, Frederick. *The Tragedy of Manners*. New Haven, CT: Yale University Press, 1957.

Donadio, Stephen. *Nietzsche, Henry James, and the Artistic Will*. New York: Oxford University Press, 1978.

Dupee, F. W. *Henry James*. New York: Sloane, 1951.

Feidleson, Charles. "The Moment of Portrait of a Lady." *Ventures* 8, No. 2 (Fall 1968): 47–55.

Fogel, Daniel Mark, ed. *A Companion to Henry James Studies*. Westport, CT: Greenwood Press, 1993.

Fowler, Virginia C. *Henry James's American Girl: The Embroidery on the Canvas*. Madison: University of Wisconsin Press, 1984.

Gale, Robert L. *The Caught Image: Figurative Language in the Fiction of Henry James*. Chapel Hill: University of North Carolina Press, 1964.

Graham, Kenneth. *Henry James: The Drama of Fulfillment*. Oxford: Clarendon Press, 1975.

Grover, Philip. *Henry James and the French Novel: A Study in Inspiration*. New York: Barnes & Noble, 1973.

Hagberg, Garry. *Meaning and Interpretation: Wittgenstein, Henry James and Literary Knowledge*. Ithaca: Cornell University Press, 1994.

Hayes, Kevin J., ed. *Henry James: The Contemporary Reviews*. New York: Cambridge University Press, 1996.

Hirsch, David H. "Henry James and the Seal of Love." *Modern Language Studies* 13, No. 4 (1983): 39–60.

Hutchinson, Stuart. *Henry James: American as Modernist*. New York: Barnes & Noble, 1982.

Jones, Granville H. *Henry James's Psychology of Experience: Innocence, Responsibility, and Renunciation in the Fiction of Henry James.* The Hague: Mouton, 1975.

Kappeler, Suzanne. *Writing and Reading Henry James.* New York: Columbia University Press, 1980.

Kaston, Carren. *Imagination and Desire in the Novels of Henry James.* New Brunswick, NJ: Rutgers University Press, 1984.

Krier, William. "The 'Latent Extravagance' of The Portrait of a Lady." *Mosaic* 9, No. 3 (1976): 57–65.

Krische, James H. *Henry James and Impressionism.* Troy, NY: Whitson, 1981.

Krook, Dorthea. *The Ordeal of Consciousness in Henry James.* Cambridge: Cambridge University Press, 1962.

Leyburn, Ellen Doublas. *Strange Alloy: The Relation of Comedy to Tragedy in the Fiction of Henry James.* Chapel Hill: University of North Carolina Press, 1968.

Long, Robert Emmet. *The Great Succession: Henry James and the Legacy of Hawthorne.* Pittsburgh: University of Pittsburgh Press, 1979.

MacKenzie, Manfred. *Communities of Honor and Love in Henry James.* Cambridge: Harvard University Press, 1976.

McMaster, Juliet. "The Portrait of Isabel Archer." *American Literature* 45 (1973): 50–66.

Norman, Ralf. *The Insecure World of Henry James's Fiction: Intensity and Ambiguity.* New York: St. Martin's Press, 1982.

O'Neill, John P. *Workable Design: Action and Situation in the Fiction of Henry James.* Port Washington, NY: Kennikat, 1973.

Perosa, Sergio. *Henry James and the Experimental Novel.* Charlottesville: University Press of Virginia, 1978.

Rimmon, Shlomith. *The Concept of Ambiguity: The Example of Henry James*. Chicago: University of Chicago Press, 1977.

Sabiston, Elizabeth. "The Prison of Womanhood." *Comparative Literature* 25 (1973): 336–51.

Schneider, Daniel J. *The Crystal Cage: Adventures of the Imagination in the Fiction of Henry James*. Lawrence: Regents Press of Kansas, 1978.

Sears, Sally. *The Negative Imagination: Form and Perspective in the Novels of Henry James*. Ithaca, NY: Cornell University Press, 1968.

Segal, Or. *The Lucid Reflector: The Observer in Henry James's Fiction*. New Haven, CT: Yale University Press, 1969.

Seltzer, Mark. *Henry James and the Art of Power*. Ithaca, NY: Cornell University Press, 1984.

Sicker, Philip. *Love and the Quest for Identity in the Fiction of Henry James*. Princeton: Princeton University Press, 1980.

Stowell, Peter H. *Literary Impressionism: James and Chekov*. Athens: University of Georgia Press, 1980.

Ward, Joseph A. *The Search for Form: Studies in the Structure of James's Fiction*. Chapel Hill: University of North Carolina Press, 1967.

Wilson, Edmund. "The Ambiguity of Henry James." In *The Tripple Thinkers*. New York: Oxford University Press, 1963, pp. 88–132.

Winner, Viola Hopkins. *Henry James and the Visual Arts*. Charlottesville: University Press of Virginia, 1970.

Index of Themes and Ideas